Guidance notes and flow charts for the

Supply Short Contract

This contract should be used for local and international procurement of goods under a single order or on a batch order basis which do not require sophisticated management techniques and impose only low risks on both the Purchaser and the Supplier

An NEC document

April 2013

NEC is a division of Thomas Telford Ltd, which is a wholly owned subsidiary of the Institution of Civil Engineers (ICE), the owner and developer of the NEC.

The NEC is a family of standard contracts, each of which has these characteristics:

- Its use stimulates good management of the relationship between the two parties to the contract and, hence, of the work included in the contract.

- It can be used in a wide variety of commercial situations, for a wide variety of types of work and in any location.

- It is a clear and simple document – using language and a structure which are straightforward and easily understood.

NEC3 Supply Short Contract is one of the NEC family and is consistent with all other NEC3 documents. Also available are the Supply Short Contract Guidance Notes and Flow Charts.

ISBN (complete box set) 978 0 7277 5867 5
ISBN (this document) 978 0 7277 5935 1
ISBN (Supply Short Contract) 978 0 7277 5897 2

First edition 2009
Reprinted 2010
Reprinted with amendments 2013

British Library Cataloguing in Publication Data for this publication is available from the British Library.

Typeset by Academic + Technical, Bristol

Printed and bound in Great Britain by Bell & Bain Limited, Glasgow, UK

CONTENTS

FOREWORD

I was delighted to be asked to write the Foreword for the NEC3 Contracts.

I have followed the outstanding rise and success of NEC contracts for a number of years now, in particular during my tenure as the 146th President of the Institution of Civil Engineers, 2010/11.

In my position as UK Government's Chief Construction Adviser, I am working with Government and industry to ensure Britain's construction sector is equipped with the knowledge, skills and best practice it needs in its transition to a low carbon economy. I am promoting innovation in the sector, including in particular the use of Building Information Modelling (BIM) in public sector construction procurement; and the synergy and fit with the collaborative nature of NEC contracts is obvious. The Government's construction strategy is a very significant investment and NEC contracts will play an important role in setting high standards of contract preparation, management and the desirable behaviour of our industry.

In the UK, we are faced with having to deliver a 15–20 per cent reduction in the cost to the public sector of construction during the lifetime of this Parliament. Shifting mind-set, attitude and behaviour into best practice NEC processes will go a considerable way to achieving this.

Of course, NEC contracts are used successfully around the world in both public and private sector projects; this trend seems set to continue at an increasing pace. NEC contracts are, according to my good friend and NEC's creator Dr Martin Barnes CBE, about better management of projects. This is quite achievable and I encourage you to understand NEC contracts to the best you can and exploit the potential this offers us all.

Peter Hansford

UK Government's Chief Construction Adviser
Cabinet Office

PREFACE

The NEC contracts are the only suite of standard contracts designed to facilitate and encourage good management of the projects on which they are used. The experience of using NEC contracts around the world is that they really make a difference. Previously, standard contracts were written mainly as legal documents best left in the desk drawer until costly and delaying problems had occurred and there were lengthy arguments about who was to blame.

The language of NEC contracts is clear and simple, and the procedures set out are all designed to stimulate good management. Foresighted collaboration between all the contributors to the project is the aim. The contracts set out how the interfaces between all the organisations involved will be managed – from the client through the designers and main contractors to all the many subcontractors and suppliers.

Versions of the NEC contract are specific to the work of professional service providers such as project managers and designers, to main contractors, to subcontractors and to suppliers. The wide range of situations covered by the contracts means that they do not need to be altered to suit any particular situation.

The NEC contracts are the first to deal specifically and effectively with management of the inevitable risks and uncertainties which are encountered to some extent on all projects. Management of the expected is easy, effective management of the unexpected draws fully on the collaborative approach inherent in the NEC contracts.

Most people working on projects using the NEC contracts for the first time are hugely impressed by the difference between the confrontational characteristics of traditional contracts and the teamwork engendered by the NEC. The NEC does not include specific provisions for dispute avoidance. They are not necessary. Collaborative management itself is designed to avoid disputes and it really works.

It is common for the final account for the work on a project to be settled at the time when the work is finished. The traditional long period of expensive professional work after completion to settle final payments just is not needed.

The NEC contracts are truly a massive change for the better for the industries in which they are used.

Dr Martin Barnes CBE

Originator of the NEC contracts

ACKNOWLEDGEMENTS

The first edition of the Supply Short Contract was produced by the Institution of Civil Engineers through its NEC Panel. It was mainly drafted by J. J. Lofty and P. A. Baird with the assistance of N. C. Shaw and J. M. Hawkins.

The NEC3 Supply Short Contract Guidance Notes were mainly drafted by J. J. Lofty with the assistance of members of the NEC Panel.

The NEC3 Supply Short Contract Flow Charts were produced by Ross Hayes.

The original NEC was designed and drafted by Dr Martin Barnes then of Coopers and Lybrand with the assistance of Professor J. G. Perry then of the University of Birmingham, T. W. Weddell then of Travers Morgan Management, T. H. Nicholson, Consultant to the Institution of Civil Engineers, A. Norman then of the University of Manchester Institute of Science and Technology and P. A. Baird, then Corporate Contracts Consultant, Eskom, South Africa.

The members of the NEC Panel are:

N. C. Shaw, FCIPS, CEng, MIMechE (Chairman)
F. Alderson, BA (Melb), Solicitor
P. A. Baird, BSc, CEng, FICE, M(SA)ICE, MAPM
M. Codling, BSc, ICIOB, MAPM
L. T. Eames, BSc, FRICS, FCIOB
M. Garratt, BSc(Hons), MRICS, FCIArb
J. J. Lofty, MRICS

NEC Consultant:

R. A. Gerrard, BSc(Hons), FRICS, FCIArb, FCInstCES

Secretariat:

J. M. Hawkins, BA(Hons), MSc
S. Hernandez, BSc, MSc

AMENDMENTS

Full details of all amendments are available on www.neccontract.com.

AMENDMENTS

INTRODUCTION

| The notes in boxes like this one | printed within the NEC3 Supply Short Contract (SSC) explain how to complete the SSC when it is used for a simple, low risk contract. These boxed notes are reproduced in these guidance notes, which also explain the background to the SSC and give guidance for its use as a main contract. Supplementary guidance is also given on how to use the SSC as a subcontract. The flow charts show the procedural logic on which the SSC is based and are published in this volume for reference.

In these guidance notes, as in the contract itself, terms which are defined in the SSC have capital initials and those which are identified in the Contract Data are in italics. The guidance notes and the flow charts are not part of the SSC and have no legal function.

WHEN TO USE THE SSC

The SSC is a contract for a *Supplier* to provide *goods*, sourced from anywhere in the world, for routine, day to day or any other purpose where the value/risk is low and does not require active management during the supply process or justify the cost of developing a detailed contract strategy. It uses established NEC principles and words as much as possible. It is designed for the supply of *goods* – not for managing a project.

The introduction of the SSC will allow existing users of the NEC system to have access to conditions of contract, for straightforward purchases, that are written in terms common to other NEC contracts, and encourage co-operative working down the supply chain.

The SSC is not limited to any particular industry and can be used in almost any sector of commercial activity. Examples of use of the SSC may be for the purchase of:

- Stationery
- Printer supplies
- Laboratory chemicals
- Tools
- Desks, chairs
- Portable test equipment
- Raw materials
- Pre manufactured materials or plant

Users choosing between the SSC and the NEC3 Supply Contract (SC) should base their choice on the level of complexity of the *goods*, the amount of active management required and the level of risk to each of the Parties.

The SSC is designed to allow the *Purchaser* the flexibility of choosing whether he wants the supply of the *goods* as a single order, which is achieved when the contract is awarded or on a Batch Order basis. This decision is made by the *Purchaser* and stated in the Contract Data.

The *Purchaser* may require the Batch Order flexibility because when he places the contract he may not yet know

- the dates when the *goods* are required,
- the exact quantities of *goods* needed for his operations or to meet the requirements of a construction project or
- both of the above.

Users should note that if the Batch Order option is not chosen it would not be possible to revert to a Batch Order basis later on as the contract in this case will be on a single order basis.

If flexibility is required when the contract is placed, the Batch Order basis should be chosen even if, eventually, only a single batch of *goods* is ordered. (See the notes on clause 23.1).

NEC3 contracts

The current list of published NEC3 contracts is stated below:

- NEC3 Engineering and Construction Contract (ECC)
- NEC3 Engineering and Construction Subcontract (ECS)
- NEC3 Engineering and Construction Short Contract (ECSC)
- NEC3 Engineering and Construction Short Subcontract (ECSS)
- NEC3 Professional Services Contract (PSC)
- NEC3 Professional Services Short Contract (PSSC)
- NEC3 Term Service Contract (TSC)
- NEC3 Term Service Short Contract (TSSC)
- NEC3 Supply Contract (SC)
- NEC3 Supply Short Contract (SSC)
- NEC3 Framework Contract (FC)
- NEC3 Adjudicator's Contract (AC)

For general guidance on when to use each contract refer to the NEC3 Procurement and Contract Strategies guide, available on www.neccontract.com.

THE SSC PACKAGE

The SSC package includes the conditions of contract and forms which, when filled in, make up a complete contract. The forms are on pages 1 to 8 of the package and are provided for

- the title page and the Contract Forms comprising
  - Contract Data,
  - The *Supplier*'s Offer,
  - The *Purchaser*'s Acceptance,
  - Price Schedule and
  - Goods Information.

Stage A: How a *Purchaser* invites tenders for *goods*

Examples using a fictitious purchase of *goods* are appended to these notes to illustrate how the title page, Contract Data, The *Supplier*'s Offer and The *Purchaser*'s Acceptance should be filled in at each of the three stages leading to a contract.

The *Purchaser* uses the package to invite tenders for the proposed purchase of *goods* by providing the following information on the forms and sending the package to tenderers with the invitation to tender.

- **The title page (page 1) – see example A1**
- **Contract Data (pages 2 and 3) – see example A2**
- **The *Supplier*'s Offer and the *Purchaser*'s Acceptance (page 4) – leave blank**
- **Price Schedule (page 5) – see notes on clause 50.3**

> Entries in the first four columns of this Price Schedule are made either by the *Purchaser* or the tenderer. If the *Supplier* is to be paid an amount for the item which is not adjusted if the quantity of *goods* in the item changes, the tenderer enters the amount in the Price column only, the Unit, Quantity and Rate columns being left blank.
>
> If the *Supplier* is to be paid an amount for the item of *goods* which is the rate for the *goods* multiplied by the quantity supplied, the tenderer enters a rate for each item and multiplies it by the Quantity to produce the Price, to be entered in the final column.

- **Goods Information (pages 6–8) (see notes on clauses 11.2(5) and 60.1(1)).**

> The Goods Information should be a complete and precise statement of the *Purchaser*'s requirements. If it is incomplete or imprecise there is a risk that the *Supplier* will interpret it differently from the *Purchaser*'s intention. Information describing the *Purchaser*'s requirements for the supply of the *goods*, including the information to be provided by the *Supplier* in connection with the supply of the *goods*, should be stated in the section headed Supply requirements.

1 Description of the *goods*

> Give a detailed description of what *goods* the *Supplier* is required to supply. This may include drawings. Give the information of the required quality standards, the tests and the inspections required and any health and safety requirements.

2 Specifications

> List the specifications that apply to this contract.

It is important that the description of the *goods* and the specifications are thoroughly prepared and comprehensive because the SSC definition of a Defect (clause 11.2(1)) is based entirely on the Goods Information. The information here should state any technical requirements for the *goods* and include

- quality standards for the *goods* and workmanship,
- any tests and inspection procedures required and
- any health and safety requirements.

The *Purchaser*'s requirements for the supply of the *goods* (including transport) are stated in the Supply requirements section of the Goods Information.

The Goods Information must identify the items of *goods* as being subject to marking under the contract and state how the marking is to be done, listing any documentation that may also be required. (See clause 71.1).

3 Constraints on how the *Supplier* Provides the Goods

> State any constraints on how the *Supplier* is to provide the *goods* such as, any limits on subcontracting.

While it is likely that most of the work to supply the *goods* will not be subcontracted as the *Purchaser* will contract directly with the *Supplier* of the *goods*, the *Supplier* should be allowed to subcontract without any limit (clause 21.1). However, the *Purchaser* may wish to limit the extent of subcontracting if, for example the *Supplier* is being selected for a particular expertise.

4 Requirements for the programme

> State whether a programme is required and, if it is, state what form it is to be in, what information is to be shown on it, when it is to be submitted and when it is to be updated.

The programme may take the form of a list of dates or a bar chart.

The information to be shown on the programme should include at least

- the *starting date*,
- the Delivery Date,
- the *Supplier*'s plan for Delivery,
- key dates for the *Purchaser* to provide "services and other things" (not earlier than the dates stated in part 5 of the Goods Information) and
- key dates for the co-ordination with other contracts (if any).

5 Services and other things provided by the *Purchaser*

> Describe what the *Purchaser* will provide, in connection with the supply of the *goods*, such as transport, loading or unloading of the *goods*.

The services the *Purchaser* provides will depend on the nature of the *goods* he is purchasing, what the *goods* are for and the delivery place where he wants Delivery of the *goods*. The services may include

- contracting for transport,
- paying the costs of transport,
- arranging access to the delivery place,
- loading and unloading the *goods* and
- undertaking any requirements for export and import.

6 Supply requirements

> State the information which describes the *Purchaser*'s requirements (other than services he is to provide) in connection with the supply of the *goods* including the requirements for transport, the mode of transport and the loading and unloading of the *goods*.
>
> State the delivery place, the hours of access to the delivery place and other information to be provided by the *Supplier* at the time of Delivery such as the delivery note, which notifies the actual delivery date. The information necessary for a purchase that involves international, cross border transactions should be stated here, such as export and import requirements of the Customs authorities.

The SSC requires users to prescribe the Supply requirements separately to ensure the matters related to the processes of supply of the *goods*, as well as the description of the *goods* themselves (see part 1 above), are clear regarding the actions, costs and risks between the Parties.

The *Purchaser* should state the extent to which the *Supplier* transports the *goods*, the mode of transport and the delivery place location (such as the *Purchaser*'s premises or another location from which the *Purchaser* may collect the *goods*.) Also state the actions of the *Supplier* during supply (such as loading and unloading the *goods* and checking packing and marking before dispatch).

The statements provided here must co-ordinate with those services the *Purchaser* will provide (see part 5 above).

- **Invitation to tender**

The *Purchaser*'s invitation to tender may, in addition to the SSC package, include details of tender return dates and the details of the person to whom queries should be addressed.

Stage B: How a tenderer makes an offer

A tenderer uses the package to make an offer by providing information on the following forms.

- Price Schedule (page 5) – see notes under stage A and on clause 50.3.
- The *Supplier*'s Offer (page 4) – see example B1.

> Enter the total of the Prices from the Price Schedule.

Additional information as part of the offer may include

- any extra Goods Information proposed by the tenderer and
- the names and particulars of the tenderer's staff proposed.

Stage C: How a contract is made

The package becomes a complete contract document when the *Purchaser* makes the following additional entries and sends a copy to the *Supplier* who has made the chosen offer.

- The *Purchaser*'s Acceptance of the offer (page 4) – see example C1.
- The title page (page 1) – *Supplier*'s name added – see example C2.
- The Contract Forms including the Contract Data (pages 2–3).

Under the law of England and Wales, the contract between the *Purchaser* and the *Supplier* is then made. There may be other requirements in other jurisdictions.

The SSC uses a simple offer (The *Supplier*'s Offer, page 4) and acceptance (The *Purchaser*'s Acceptance, page 4) to create a contract. It is emphasised that this is the most efficient and clear way of creating a simple contract and users should aim to achieve this. However, if

- the tenderer requires changes to the documents or
- the *Purchaser* has issued supplements to the invitation to tender amending the documents,

these need to be recorded. This is achieved by additional entries in the Contract Data. Extensive additional entries should be avoided.

It must be emphasised that it is good practice for a *Purchaser* to issue enquiry packages that are properly described and not unreasonable or difficult to fulfill in the prevailing circumstances, conversely tenderer's should avoid requiring changes unless it is necessary to avoid uncertainty or unreasonable risk.

NOTES ON THE CLAUSES

1 General

Action **10**

10.1   The first statement in this clause obliges the *Purchaser* and the *Supplier* to do everything which the contract states they are to do. It is the only clause which uses the future tense. For simplicity, everything else is in the present tense. Where actions are permitted but not obligatory, the term 'may' is used.

The other statement obliges how the parties act. This is a fundamental requirement of all contracts in the NEC family and is designed to encourage a collaborative rather than a confrontational approach to management of the contract.

Identified and **11**
defined terms

11.1   The Contract Data is used to complete the contract by identifying terms in italics and providing the information that certain clauses state is in the Contract Data (see examples A2 and B1). The definitions used in the contract are given in clause 11.

11.2(1)   Any departure from the *goods* as described in the Goods Information constitutes a Defect.

11.2(2)   This definition of Defined Cost, which is used in the assessment of a compensation event, includes four basic components. Defined Cost is the cost of the components listed for work done by the *Supplier* and his subcontractors.

Allowable payments made by the *Supplier* do not include recoverable tax. This is added when the *Supplier* is paid the amount due under clause 50.3. Otherwise all payments made for a resource should be included subject to clause 63.3.

11.2(3)   The Goods Information should state what *goods* the *Supplier* is required to supply and how he is to supply them to achieve Delivery; disputes can arise if this is not done clearly and unambiguously. This provides flexibility for the *Purchaser* to specify Delivery at the level he requires. Delivery is therefore a defined state and not a date. It is when the *Purchaser* decides the *Supplier* has met all the requirements, in the Goods Information, for Delivery.

The *Purchaser* should consider carefully how he wants to define when Delivery is achieved and put that in the Goods Information. He should also state the requirements in connection with the supply of the *goods* including what documentation the *Supplier* is to provide before Delivery is achieved.

11.2(4)   The Delivery Date is the date by which the *Supplier* is contractually obliged to achieve Delivery of the *goods* – clause 30.1.

The *delivery date* is stated in the Contract Data. It may be changed in various ways under the SSC, for example as a consequence of a compensation event or an instruction from the *Purchaser* – clause 14.2.

If the Batch Order option is chosen the *delivery date* for the *goods* in the batch is stated in the Batch Order – see notes on clause 23.1.

11.2(5)   Goods Information is information which specifies what *goods* the *Supplier* is to provide. It can be in the form of a specification and drawings. The Goods Information also sets out any constraints on how the *Supplier* Provides the

Goods. Further advice on the contents of Goods Information is given under "Stage A: How a *Purchaser* invites tenders for *goods*" earlier in these Guidance Notes.

11.2(7) The Prices are the basis on which the amount due is calculated and may comprise both lump sums and quantified items.

11.2(8) The definition of "To Provide the Goods", in conjunction with the definition of Goods Information 11.2(5), identifies the *Supplier*'s main obligation in clause 20.1.

Interpretation and the law 12

12.3 Orally agreed changes to the contract have no effect unless they are followed up by the procedures stated in this clause.

Communications 13

13.2 The *period of reply*, stated by the *Purchaser* in the Contract Data (example A2), aims to achieve a timely turn round of communications. Its length depends on the circumstances of the contract but would normally be two or three weeks. Other periods for specific actions are stated in the relevant clauses (for example clause 62.1 – submission of quotations for compensation events). All such periods can be changed only by agreement between the Parties.

The *Purchaser*'s authority and delegation 14

14.1 Only the *Purchaser*, or an authorised delegate of the *Purchaser* (clause 14.4), can change the Goods Information.

14.2 The *Purchaser* may instruct a change to the Delivery Date, but only after consultation with the *Supplier*. The intention of the consultation is to discuss the reason for the *Purchaser*'s requirement and the implications this may have for the *Supplier*. If the change to the Delivery Date is instructed this is a compensation event (see clause 60.1(2)).

14.3 This clause makes clear that acceptance by the *Purchaser* of the *Supplier*'s communication or of his work does not result in a transfer of the *Supplier*'s responsibility to Provide the Goods.

14.4 The *Purchaser* may wish to delegate any of his actions, for example to a supply manager.

Access and the provision of services 15

15.1 The *Purchaser* is required to allow access to and use of the *premises* identified in the Contract Data as necessary for the work included in this contract.

15.2 Refer to the notes on Goods Information part 5 under 'Stage A: How a *Purchaser* invites tenders for *goods*' earlier in these Guidance Notes.

Early Warning 16

16.1 The obligation which this clause requires of both Parties is intended to bring into the open as early as possible any matter which could adversely affect the successful outcome of the contract. Both Parties should give early warning in order to maximise the time available for taking avoiding action.

16.2 The Parties are required to co-operate in giving priority to solving the problem, irrespective of how the problem has been caused and who carries the financial responsibility for it. Any discussion between the Parties should concentrate on solving the problem. The purpose of the Parties' discussion is not to decide responsibility or who will pay for the actions taken; the relevant provisions of the contract will cover these aspects.

2 The *Supplier*'s main responsibilities

Providing the Goods	**20**	
	20.1	This clause states the *Supplier*'s basic obligation. "Provide the Goods" is defined in clause 11.2(8). It includes providing all necessary resources to achieve the end result. These clauses demonstrate the importance of thoroughly prepared and comprehensive Goods Information (see the notes on Goods Information under Stage A: How a *Purchaser* invites tenders for *goods*).
Subcontracting	**21**	
	21.1 & 21.2	As in other NEC contracts, the SSC does not provide for nominated subcontractors. The *Supplier* has full responsibility for Providing the Goods, whether subcontracted or not (see the notes on Goods Information part 3 under Stage A: How a *Purchaser* invites tenders for *goods*).
Other responsibilities	**22**	
	22.2	Various clauses in the contract give the *Purchaser* authority to issue instructions to the *Supplier*. These instructions should be given within the time limits and for the reasons stated. The *Supplier* should always obey the instruction and if for any reason he disagrees with an instruction the procedures in the contract should be used for dealing with the situation.
	22.3	The *Supplier* is required to obtain permission from others, if necessary, before transporting the *goods*. This obligation will depend on the Supply requirements stated by the *Purchaser* in part 6 of the Goods Information.
Batch Orders	**23**	
	23.1	This clause only applies if the *Purchaser* states in the Contract Data that he requires the *Supplier* to Provide the Goods when instructed by Batch Order (see example A2). This option is most likely to be used when the *Purchaser* requires flexibility, when the contract is made, of fixing the date he requires the *goods*.

The *Purchaser* is required to consult on the contents of a Batch Order with the *Supplier* before he issues it, this will avoid any misunderstanding. The clause sets out the information to be included on the Batch Order (see the example Batch Order with these Guidance Notes).

If the *goods* are instructed by Batch Order the *Purchaser* must enter a *delay damages* amount, appropriate to the requirements in the Batch Order, in the Contract Data. The *delay damages* amount could be based on the quantity of *goods* in the batch or some other basis appropriate to the intended use of the *goods*. It is important that the amount is a genuine pre-estimate of the damage that would be suffered by the *Purchaser* as a result of delay to providing the items of *goods* in a batch.

It is important that the period between the date of issue of each Batch Order is realistic and practicable for both Parties. The *Purchaser* identifies the *batch order interval* in the Contract Data and this can be extended or reduced if both Parties agree.

Due to the open ended nature of the batch ordering process an *end date* is stated in the Contract Data by the *Purchaser* and no Batch Orders can be issued by him after this date. The *Supplier* completes the supply of *goods* in a Batch Order instructed before the *end date*.

The Batch Order is priced from the prices for the items of *goods* in the Price Schedule which were agreed when the contract is awarded.

The Batch Order option introduces three additional compensation events to those in clause 60.1(1). These additional compensation events make clear that the *Purchaser* carries the financial risk if he orders an item of *goods* that is not included in the Price Schedule, the total quantity of *goods* ordered is different from that stated in the Price Schedule or the quantity of *goods* is outside the expected quantity range stated in the Contract Data (see example A2).

3 Time

Starting and Delivery 30

30.1   The *starting date* has several uses in the SSC

- it is the earliest date on which the *Supplier* can start the supply of the *goods* if the single order option is chosen by the *Purchaser* or the earliest date the *Purchaser* can start ordering by batch if that option is chosen,
- it determines when there is an *assessment day* for payment (clause 50.1) and
- it is the start of the period during which insurance cover is required (clause 84.1).

Refer to the notes on clauses 11.2(3) and (4), definitions of Delivery and Delivery Date respectively and also clause 14.2, changes to the Delivery Date.

Instructions to stop or 31
not start work 31.1   An instruction given under this clause is a compensation event (clause 60.1(5)). However, if the reason for the instruction arises from the fault of the *Supplier*, the Prices and the Delivery Date are not changed. In the event that the *Purchaser* fails to instruct the re-start of work within eight weeks of instructing work to stop, the *Supplier* may be entitled to terminate (clause 90.4).

The programme 32

32.1   Refer to the notes on Goods Information part 4 under Stage A: How a *Purchaser* invites tenders for *goods*.

4 Testing and Defects

Tests and inspections 40

40.1   The Goods Information should include a comprehensive specification of the standards to be achieved in the *goods*. If the *Purchaser* has specific requirements for inspection and testing, these should also be stated in the Goods Information, including the associated procedures and responsibilities for carrying out the inspections and tests. The *Supplier* is obligated to correct a Defect that is shown by the inspection or test and the inspection or test is then repeated.

Notifying Defects 41

41.1   The *defects date* is fixed by a period after Delivery stated by the *Purchaser* in the Contract Data (example A2). The length of the period will depend on the type of *goods* and their characteristics. The *Purchaser* may notify Defects at any time until the end of this period.

Correcting Defects 42

42.1 &   Before Delivery the *Supplier* must correct a Defect whether or not he is
42.2   notified of it. This can be done at any time so long as the *Supplier* meets his obligations under the contract.

After Delivery, the *Supplier* must correct the Defect within the period stated by the *Purchaser* in the Contract Data. This period is to ensure the timely correction of a Defect and should take into account the *Purchaser*'s urgency for use of the *goods* or any commitment he may have to others. The period should aim to be one that minimises the impact of the Defect on the *Purchaser*'s requirements.

Accepting Defects 43

43.1 &
43.2

Although a Defect may be minor, its correction may be costly to the *Supplier*. Correction of the Defect may also cause inconvenience to the *Purchaser* out of all proportion to the benefits gained. Additionally, correction may have become impossible because of the use the *Purchaser* has made of the *goods* or some other reason.

These clauses state the procedure in the contract for accepting a Defect in these circumstances. Either Party may propose that the Defect should be accepted. The other is not obliged to accept the proposal.

The *Supplier*'s quotation will show a reduction in the Prices or an earlier Delivery Date or both. In some cases the reduction in money and time may be nominal. If the quotation is not accepted by the *Purchaser* no further action is necessary other than to correct the Defect.

Uncorrected Defects 44

44.1

This clause applies to any notified Defect outstanding after its correction period stated in the Contract Data.

5 Payment

Assessing the amount due 50

50.1

The *Purchaser*'s statement in the Contract Data fixes an *assessment day* in each month from the *starting date* until the month after the *defects date* (see example A2). This provides for a monthly assessment by the *Supplier* even when the amount due may be nil.

50.2

The *Supplier* assesses the amount due by each *assessment day* and uses the assessment to apply to the *Purchaser* for payment.

50.3

The payment mechanism is based on the use of the Price Schedule and the Prices.

The Price Schedule included in the contract provides the pricing information needed for assessing the amount due. Notes on how to use the Price Schedule form are included under its heading in the SSC and are repeated in these notes under 'Stage A: How a *Purchaser* invites tenders for *goods*'.

The Prices are defined in clause 11.2(7). The second sentence of the definition provides for the pricing of those items for which a quantity and a rate are stated in the Price Schedule.

Payments for an item in the Price Schedule does not become due until the *goods* or work described in the item has been completed unless a quantity and a rate are stated in the Price Schedule for the item, in that case the Price for the quantity of *goods* or work in the item which has been completed is included.

These definitions and the layout of the Price Schedule provide for flexibility in tendering methods including items which

a) the *Purchaser* describes and for which the tenderer quotes a Price,
b) the *Purchaser* describes with a quantity and for which the tenderer quotes a rate extended to a Price (adjustable to quantity completed),

c) the *Purchaser* describes and the tenderer breaks down into sub-items comprising a mixture of a) and b), each of which the tenderer quotes for,

d) the *Purchaser* describes and the tenderer quotes for a list of the activities necessary to complete the item, each with a Price or

e) the tenderer describes and quotes Prices or rates in accordance with the notes at the head of the Price Schedule and the invitation to tender.

It is important that item descriptions are carefully written with appropriate references to the Goods Information, including testing requirements. For quantified items, the *goods* to be covered by the rate must be clearly stated.

The third and fourth bullets in clause 50.3 state the other amounts to be added to or deducted in order to calculate the amount due. These amounts may include damages and any VAT or sales tax. It is recommended that the Parties should agree, at the start of the contract, how the administration of sales tax documentation should be dealt with as part of the payment procedure.

No provision is made for inflation. In some countries where inflation is high the *Purchaser* may wish to take the risk of Price increases beyond a predetermined threshold. This could be provided for in additional conditions of contract.

No provision has been made for advanced payments. If the *Purchaser* is prepared to make an advanced payment, a separate item should be included in the Price Schedule. The item must describe how the advanced payment is repaid. It may also be appropriate for an additional condition of contract to provide for an early payment bond or other security.

50.5 The *delay damages* to be stated in the Contract Data (see example A2) are the amount to be paid by the *Supplier* to the *Purchaser* if the *Supplier* fails to supply the *goods* by the Delivery Date. Under the law of England and Wales, the amount of *delay damages* should not exceed a genuine pre-estimate of the damage that would be suffered by the *Purchaser* as a result of the delay to Delivery. The *Purchaser* should keep a record of the calculation of the pre-estimate if the Batch Order option is chosen then see the notes on clause 23.1.

Payment 51

51.1 The latest date for payment is related to the *assessment day* which occurs after the *Purchaser* receives the *Supplier*'s application.

51.2 For simplicity, a fixed rate of interest of 0.5% per week is stated for the calculation of interest due on late payments, with an option for the *Purchaser* to state a different rate in the Contract Data.

> Enter an interest rate only if a rate less than 0.5% per week of delay has been agreed.

6 Compensation events

Compensation events 60 As in other NEC contracts, compensation events are those events stated in the contract to be compensation events. If an event is not so stated, it is not a compensation event and is at the *Supplier*'s financial risk. If a compensation event occurs and does not arise from the *Supplier*'s fault (see clause 61.2), the *Supplier* may be compensated for any effect the event has on cost or the Delivery Date.

60.1 The events which are compensation events in the SSC are stated in this clause.

Any compensation events other than those identified in clause 60.1 that are required for a specific contract should be stated in an additional condition of contract in the Contract Data.

Any risk which it is prudent for the *Purchaser* to carry can be dealt with in this way.

60.1(1) This event embodies the principle that a tender can only be based on the information the tenderer has when the tender is prepared.

The exception is the case when the *Purchaser* is willing to accept a Defect and has agreed to change the Goods Information to accommodate it.

60.1(2) This event relates to the *Purchaser*'s authority in clause 14.2 to change the Delivery Date.

60.1(3) This event relates to the *Purchaser*'s obligation in clause 15.1 to allow access to and use of the *premises* stated in the Contract Data.

60.1(4) This event relates to the *Purchaser*'s failure to provide the services and other things as stated in the Goods Information (see clause 15.2).

60.1(5) This event relates to the *Purchaser*'s authority in clause 31.1 to stop or not start work.

60.1(6) This event relates to the *Purchaser*'s obligation in clause 13.2 to reply to a communication within stated periods.

60.1(7) The *Purchaser* is able to change a decision made under the contract.

60.1(8) The *Purchaser*'s risks are stated in clause 80.1.

Notifying **61**
compensation events 61.1 Either the *Purchaser* or the *Supplier* can notify a compensation event to the other; this clause limits when the *Supplier* can do so. The *Purchaser* should instruct the *Supplier* to submit a quotation at the same time as notifying a compensation event to the *Supplier*.

The stated time limit is intended to expedite the procedure so that dealing with compensation events a long time after they have occurred is avoided.

61.2 This clause states the actions to be taken by the *Purchaser* within one week of a compensation event being notified by the *Supplier*. If the *Purchaser* decides that one of the four stated criteria applies, the compensation event procedure does not continue.

61.3 This relates to the early warning procedure in clause 16.1 and to clause 63.5 (see the notes on clause 63.5).

Quotations for **62**
compensation events 62.1 This clause describes what a quotation for a compensation event is to comprise and states the periods within which the *Supplier* is required to submit it.

62.2 If the *Purchaser* is considering an action which would be a compensation event (such as a possible change to the *goods* or a Batch Order requiring a change to the *goods*), the *Purchaser* is able to instruct the *Supplier* to submit a quotation for the proposed event without instructing the action. The *Purchaser* can decide whether or not to proceed with the action on receipt of the quotation (see clause 62.3).

62.3 If the *Supplier* fails to provide a quotation within two weeks, as is required by clause 62.1, the *Purchaser* notifies his own assessment of the compensation event. In that case if the *Supplier* is dissatisfied with the assessment he refers it to the *Adjudicator*.

62.4 This clause states the alternative replies open to the *Purchaser* and the time within which they are to be given.

If the *Purchaser* accepts a quotation, the Prices and the Delivery Date are changed in accordance with it and the contract proceeds on that new basis having taken account of the compensation event.

	62.5	This clause states a procedure to follow if the *Purchaser* does not agree with a quotation, culminating in the *Purchaser* notifying the *Supplier* of his own assessment. In the meantime, the *Supplier* is obligated to carry out the *Purchaser*'s instruction (clause 22.2).

Assessing compensation events **63** Clause 63 states how the effects of compensation events on the Prices and the Delivery Date are assessed. This is the same whether the assessment is done by the *Supplier*, the *Purchaser* or the *Adjudicator*. The methods of assessing the changes to the Prices or rates are dealt with in clauses 63.1, 63.2 and 63.3 and of assessing a delay to the Delivery Date in clause 63.4.

63.1 This clause describes the assessment procedure used when the compensation event only affects the quantities of *goods* shown in the Price Schedule for which a quantity and rate are stated. For simplicity, if the *Purchaser* and the *Supplier* agree, the rates in the Price Schedule are used to price the changed quantities.

63.2 This clause states the procedure used for all other compensation events and should be read in conjunction with clause 63.3 and the definition of Defined Cost in clause 11.2(2).

The effect of the compensation event on the Defined Cost is assessed as the forecast for work in providing the *goods* yet to be done, it will include an element, as recorded, for any work which has already been done. (See notes on clause 11.2(2)).

The percentage for overheads and profit quoted in the *Supplier*'s Offer (see the notes on 'Stage B: How a tenderer makes an offer' and example B1) are applied to any change in the Defined Cost due to the compensation event. The percentage is required to cover all costs and overheads not included in the Defined Cost as well as an allowance for profit.

63.3 Defined Cost is defined in clause 11.2(2). This clause states how Defined Cost is established and states the deductions made from it in the assessment of the effects of compensation events.

63.4 If the *Supplier*'s planned Delivery is delayed by the forecast effect of a compensation event, the Delivery Date is delayed by the same period. If planned Delivery is not delayed, the Delivery Date is unchanged.

63.5 This clause encourages the *Supplier* to give early warnings and makes clear that the opportunity lost through the *Supplier* not giving an early warning will be used in the assessment of the compensation event.

63.6 Allowances for risk are to be included in forecasts of Defined Cost and Delivery in the same way that the *Supplier* allows for them when pricing the tender.

The cost of preparing quotations for a compensation event is specifically excluded from the assessment of that compensation event. The *Contractor* should therefore allow for these costs in his percentage for overheads and profits he quotes in the *Contractor*'s Offer in the Contract Data.

63.7 This clause protects the *Purchaser* against inefficiency on the part of the *Supplier*.

63.8 This value of compensation events are added to the Price Schedule.

63.9 This clause emphasises the finality of the assessment of compensation events. If the forecast of the effect on Defined Cost or delay to Delivery included in the accepted or notified assessment proves to be wrong when the work in providing the *goods* is done, the assessment is not changed.

7 Title

The *Purchaser*'s title to the *goods*	**70**	
	70.1	This clause makes clear that title to the *goods* only passes from the *Supplier* to the *Purchaser* before the *goods* are brought within the delivery place if the *Supplier* has marked them for this contract. The *Supplier*'s obligation to mark the *goods* is set out in clause 71.1.
	70.2	This clause makes clear that title to the *goods* passes from the *Supplier* to the *Purchaser* when the *goods* are brought within the delivery place.
Marking *goods* before Delivery	**71**	
	71.1	The Goods Information must identify the items as being subject to marking under the contract and state how the marking is to be done, listing any documentation that may also be required. Typical practice would be to label the *goods* with a statement that they are the property of the *Purchaser* in terms of the contract. A separate item could be included in the Price Schedule for this activity. The Goods Information should state not only how the *Supplier* is to mark the *goods*, but also how the marking will be verified to the *Purchaser* before payment is processed.

8 Risks, indemnities, insurance and liability

Purchaser's risks	**80**	It is important to recognise the distinction between the various types of risk and which Party bears them. Risks of loss of or physical damage to property or of personal injury or death, which are usually insurable risks, are quite separate from general, legal or financial risks.
		The clauses in this section deal with the general, legal and the insurable risks of loss, damage, injury or death and what insurances are required to cover them. The risks which could result in loss, damage, injury or death, if they happen, are allocated to either the *Purchaser* or the *Supplier*.
		Financial risks are dealt with in clause 86 (limitation of liability) and in other parts of the contract, such as under the compensation event procedure in section 6. For example, the *Purchaser* carries the financial risk for additional *goods* instructed under clause 60.1(1) but the risk in supply of the *goods* remains with the *Supplier*. In addition, the *Purchaser* carries the financial risk if any events that are at his risk occur – see clause 60.1(8).
		On the other hand, the *Supplier* carries the financial risk of doing work which he has priced in the contract.
	80.1	The *Purchaser*'s risks are stated in clause 80.1. There are three categories of *Purchaser*'s risks.
		The first is the *Purchaser*'s risks relating to the outcome of the supply of the *goods* and his own general or legal responsibilities.
		The second and third categories of *Purchaser*'s risk are the loss of or damage to the *goods* after Delivery and any retained by the *Purchaser* if a termination occurs after Delivery. There are some important risks which, even after Delivery, remain with the *Supplier*, but these are likely to be small and cease at the *defects date*.
The *Supplier*'s risks	**81**	
	81.1	The *Supplier*'s risks are defined as all the risks which are not identified in clause 80.1 as being carried by the *Purchaser*. At first reading this looks like a daunting prospect for the *Supplier*, but in reality is no different to the risks he always carries in the course of his business, unless he excludes certain risks expressly. In any case the majority of risk is passed to the *Purchaser* at Delivery.

Loss of and damage to the goods	**82** 82.1	The *Supplier* is required to carry out all activities of repair to the *goods* until the *defects date*. Consequently, unless otherwise instructed by the *Purchaser*, this will include repairs arising from a *Purchaser*'s risk event, such as damage to the *goods* after Delivery but before the *defects date*. The carrying out of such work will be a compensation event – see clause 60.1(8).

The *Purchaser* must therefore decide how to deal with loss or damage caused by a *Purchaser*'s risk event. It is possible that, in certain circumstances, he decides the damage should not be repaired, or should be repaired by the *Purchaser* or others employed by him. In such a case he would issue instructions to the *Supplier*, who will then neither be obliged to carry out such repair activities nor be entitled to receive any compensation.

Indemnity	**83** 83.1 & 83.2	Under these clauses each Party indemnifies the other for events which are at his risk. This includes all types of risk as identified above. Provision is made for the liability of a Party to be reduced on a proportional basis if events at the risk of the other Party contributed to the event.

Insurance cover	**84** 84.1	This clause requires the *Supplier* to take out insurance cover to the extent stated, from the *starting date* until the *defects* date; this is except for any insurance which the *Purchaser* provides as stated in the Contract Data.

Insurance policies	**85** 85.1	The Parties have the option of requesting the other to provide certificates confirming the required insurances are in place.

Limitation of liability	**86**	This clause places limits on various liabilities that the *Supplier* may have to the *Purchaser* arising under or in connection with the contract and addresses three key liabilities. It can also provide overall caps, in terms of both time and money, beyond which the *Supplier* has no further liability to the *Purchaser*.

Flexibility has been maintained by the use of amounts stated in the Contract Data for each cap, which can vary from 'nil' to whatever amount the Parties are prepared to accept. If the *Purchaser* wants to use some, but not all, of the provisions of this clause he can insert the word 'unlimited' against those matters that he does not wish to cap.

Users are advised to seek legal advice relating to the law under which the contract is to be made in order to be aware of how these provisions and the amounts used may be applied under that law.

	86.1	This clause limits the *Supplier*'s exposure to what are commonly referred to as consequential or indirect losses incurred by the *Purchaser*. There is not a common acceptance in all jurisdictions on the exact meaning of these terms, but neither is there clearer common term to limit the *Supplier*'s liability to damages such as loss of profit or business opportunity that are outside of his control (and sometimes of disproportionate magnitude to the value of the contract). If in doubt legal advice should be sought.
	86.2	If the *Supplier* is required to work within or adjacent to the *Purchaser*'s facility, such as when unloading *goods*, the *Supplier* is exposed to risks arising from damage he may cause to such a facility. The *Purchaser*'s costs arising from such an incident could be many times greater than the value of the contract, or of the insurance which either Party may have arranged either under the contract or otherwise. This clause limits the claim the *Purchaser* may make against the *Supplier* for his costs.
	86.3	This clause confirms that the limits apply irrespective of whether the *Purchaser* is making the claim under the contract, in tort (or delict in some jurisdictions) or in terms of any other right the *Purchaser* might have under the law of the contract.

9 Termination and dispute resolution

Termination and reasons for termination	**90**	
	90.1	Both the *Purchaser* and *Supplier* have rights to terminate the *Supplier* obligations under the contract in certain circumstances. This termination does not terminate the contract itself. The *Purchaser* is obliged to issue a termination certificate if either Party wishes to terminate in accordance with clauses 90.2, 90.3, 90.4 or 90.5. The *Supplier* then does no further work to Provide the Goods.
	90.2 to 90.5	The *Purchaser* may terminate for the reasons stated and for any reason. The *Supplier* may terminate only for the particular reasons stated.
Procedures on termination	**91**	
	91.1	The *Purchaser* will secure title to any *goods* when the *Purchaser* has paid for them. This will be achieved by payment on termination (see clause 92.1).
	91.2	The *Supplier* is only required to return equipment and surplus things to the *Purchaser*.
Payment on termination	**92**	
	92.1	This clause lists the components that are always included in the amount due on termination.
		When assessing the cost of plant and materials care must be taken to ensure that there is no duplication with any amount that is assessed as being due for normal payments.
	92.2	This clause states further components which are included in the amount due when termination has occurred for particular reasons. They reflect the different reasons for termination.
		Reason 8 is deliberately not mentioned in this clause. If Reason 8 is the cause of termination, the amount due is only that stated in clause 92.1.
Dispute resolution	**93**	
	93.1	This clause establishes the principle, followed in other NEC contracts, that any dispute which cannot be resolved by the Parties themselves must be decided by the *Adjudicator* who is independent of the Parties and is required to act impartially.
		It is important for the Parties to understand that both dispute resolution processes should only be used after attempts at negotiations have failed. They should not be seen as an alternative to the Parties reaching agreement on their disputes, either through informal negotiation, or via other more formal non-binding processes such as mediation or conciliation. Such negotiations will usually need to take place within a short time period because of the limited time available to refer a dispute to the *Adjudicator* in clause 93.3(1). However the Parties can change the contract to extend this time limit by an agreement recorded in accordance with clause 12.3, if they feel that more time is needed for resolving the dispute. If the referral is not made within the time stated or if that time is not extended by agreement, the Parties may no longer dispute the matter.
The *Adjudicator*	93.2(1)	The person appointed as *Adjudicator* should normally be named in the Contract Data. The *Adjudicator's* impartiality and independence must be ensured. For larger value contracts, it is recommended that possible names are suggested by the *Purchaser* in the invitation to tender so that the *Supplier* can agree a name for inclusion in the final Contract Data. Acceptance of the *Supplier's* Offer signifies agreement to the named *Adjudicator*.

The *Adjudicator* should be a person with practical experience of the kind of *goods* to be provided by the *Supplier*. The *Adjudicator* should be able to

- understand the procedures embodied in the SSC,
- understand the roles of both the *Purchaser* and the *Supplier* in the SSC,
- act impartially and in a spirit of independence of the Parties,
- understand and have access to costs at current market rates,
- understand and have access to information on planning times and productivities and
- appreciate risks and how allowances for them should be set.

The *Adjudicator* should be willing to obtain other specialist advice when required.

Under the NEC Adjudicator's Contract the *Adjudicator* is appointed jointly by the Parties. Unless the Parties agree otherwise, his charges (fees and expenses) are shared equally between the Parties, regardless of the *Adjudicator's* decision on the dispute.

93.2(2) This clause makes provision for the appointment of an *Adjudicator* when necessary. This will be because one was not identified in the Contract Data, or the originally chosen *Adjudicator* is no longer able to act. Initially, the Parties should try to reach agreement on a suitable person. If they cannot agree, the *Adjudicator nominating body* named in the Contract Data will make the choice for them. In the UK, the professional institutions have lists of adjudicators from which the *Adjudicator* may be selected.

The adjudication 93.3(1) In order to ensure the early declaration of a dispute and expedite its resolution, time limits are stated. After notification of a dispute a minimum of two weeks (maximum four weeks) has to elapse before the dispute can be referred to the *Adjudicator*. This is intended to allow and encourage the Parties to resolve the dispute themselves. Compliance with the time periods stated in this clause is crucially important otherwise the dispute is barred from referral to the *Adjudicator*.

93.3(2) & (3) These clauses set time limits for providing to the *Adjudicator*, and allow the *Adjudicator* to issue any instructions necessary to help him in reaching a decision.

93.3(5) This clause requires the *Adjudicator* to use the procedures for assessing compensation events in clause 63 if he has to assess additional cost or delay caused to the *Supplier*.

93.3(6) The time for the *Adjudicator's* decision is fixed, but it can be extended if necessary by agreement. If the decision is not given within the time required, and no further time is agreed, a Party can act as though the *Adjudicator* had resigned. This allows the Party to have a replacement *Adjudicator* appointed under clause 93.2(2).

Review by the *tribunal* 93.4 Under clause 93.3(8) the *Adjudicator's* decision is binding unless and until it is revised by the *tribunal*. A dispute cannot be referred to the *tribunal* unless it has first been referred to the *Adjudicator*.

This clause states the circumstances in which a referral can be made with a time limit for notifying a Party's intention to do so. The *Purchaser* identifies the *tribunal* in the Contract Data (see example A2). The choice will normally be between arbitration and the courts, either being competent to give a legally final and binding decision on the dispute. It is important to be aware of the different choices that are available when making the decision about the *tribunal*. Different laws and arbitration procedures exist in different countries, whilst in some countries no arbitration exists at all. If the *tribunal* is arbitration, the arbitration procedure to be used is also stated in the Contract Data (see example A2).

JOINING SUBCONTRACT DISPUTES WITH MAIN CONTRACT DISPUTES

Under clause 21.1, the *Supplier* is responsible for all subcontractors. It is recommended that the *Adjudicator* named in the main contract is also appointed to act in all subcontracts, subject, of course, to the agreement of the subcontractor concerned.

If the *Supplier* wishes to have any matter arising under or in connection with a subcontract that impinges on a main contract matter decided with the main contract matter, the following clause should be included in the main contract.

Combining procedures 93.5 If there is a matter arising under or in connection with a subcontract to this contract which is also a matter arising under or in connection with this contract

- the *Supplier* notifies the subcontractor that the subcontractor may attend the meeting between the Parties or
- the *Supplier* may submit the subcontract matter to the *Adjudicator* at the same time as the main contract matter.

Decisions are made on the two matters together and references to the Parties include the subcontractor.

HOW TO USE THE SSC AS A SUBCONTRACT

The SSC can be used as a subcontract to the SSC or other contracts from the NEC family. If so, it will need to be adapted as suggested in the following notes, which should be read in conjunction with the main guidance notes.

Options

Use of the SSC as a subcontract ensures as far as possible that the two contracts are "back-to-back". This minimises the risk to the *Supplier* as he passes his risks to the subcontractor in respect of the work in the subcontract. If the SSC is used as a subcontract to the SSC the payment mechanism is "back-to-back". However, it is possible that the *Supplier* may be appointed as a subcontractor to a main contractor (*Purchaser*) who is appointed under another NEC contract (for example the NEC3 Engineering and Construction Contract (ECC)). The main Option in the ECC main contract may be different to the payment mechanism in the SSC. For example, the ECC main contract may be carried out under ECC Option C – target contract. This will affect such things as payment and assessment of compensation events (see below).

Identification of terms

When using the SSC as a subcontract to the SSC, the *Purchaser* named in the Contract Data for the subcontract would be the *Supplier* in the main contract. The *Supplier* named in the subcontract would be the Supplier (Y) in the subcontract. The parties to the subcontract would then be main *Supplier* as Purchaser (X) and Supplier (Y) as *Supplier* respectively.

It facilitates management of the subcontract if a person equivalent to the one in the main contract is appointed in the subcontract.

To avoid confusion, in these notes, the terms set out in the table below are used.

SSC main contract	*Purchaser*	*Supplier*	
SSC as subcontract		*Purchaser*	*Supplier*
Terms used in this guidance note	*Purchaser*	Purchaser (X)	Supplier (Y)

The *Adjudicator* in the subcontract should be appointed in the same way as in the main contract.

Goods Information

The Purchaser (X) should prepare the Goods Information for the subcontract thoroughly to ensure that the subcontracted *goods* is properly undertaken by the Supplier (Y) in accordance with the requirements of the main contract.

The following information about the main contract should be included in the subcontract.

- Title of the main contract Supply (Goods).
- Name of the main contract *Purchaser*.

Supplier (Y's) programme

The Purchaser (X) should ensure that the information (dates, timing, etc.) which he requires to be shown on the Supplier (Y's) programme is consistent with, and is such as to enable him to comply with, his own programme and other obligations in the main contract. These requirements should be included in the Subcontract Goods Information.

Payment

The payment mechanism is the Price Schedule which is the same for both the main contract and the subcontract therefore the arrangement is "back-to-back". The amount paid to the Supplier (Y) is for the *goods* in the Subcontract Price Schedule which the Supplier (Y) has carried out. Defined Cost in the main contract includes payments for 'subcontracted work' and this is used for the assessment of compensation events (see below).

Compensation events

In order to allow adequate time for the involvement of Supplier (Y) in the assessment of a compensation event which affects the main contract, careful consideration should be given to adjustment of the time periods. The following additional conditions of contract, which are suggested as a guide, should be entered in the Contract Data for the subcontract.

"In these conditions of contract the periods of time in the clauses stated are changed as follows:

- clause 61.1, second sentence, 'four weeks' is changed to 'three weeks'.
- clause 61.2, last sentence, 'one week' is changed to 'two weeks'.
- clause 62.1, third sentence, 'two weeks' is changed to 'one week'.
- clause 62.3, 'two weeks' is changed to 'four weeks'.
- clause 62.5, first sentence, 'two weeks' is changed to 'four weeks'."

Disputes

A provision should be included to cater for a dispute arising under the main contract which concerns the subcontract. This enables the Purchaser (X) to require that such a dispute can be dealt with jointly with the dispute under the main contract by the main contract *Adjudicator*. This avoids two different adjudicators making different decisions on the same dispute.

The subcontract *Adjudicator* may be a person different from the main contract *Adjudicator*. His function is to deal with disputes which arise only between the Purchaser (X) and Supplier (Y) and which do not concern the *Purchaser*.

If any of the three parties to a joint dispute disagrees with the *Adjudicator*'s decision, he may refer it to the tribunal, as in the case of a dispute between only two contracting parties.

Insurance

By providing part of the *goods* as a subcontract, the *Supplier* in effect, passes to the Supplier (Y) those of the *Supplier*'s risks under the main contract which apply to work in the subcontract. Double insurance is largely avoided since the insurance premiums payable by the *Supplier* under the main contract will reflect the proportion of the *goods* which is subcontracted.

PROJECT BANK ACCOUNT

The *Supplier* may be included in the Project Bank Account (PBA) arrangements in the *Purchaser*'s contract with his employer. If so, the following clauses and Deeds should be included as an additional condition in the Contract Data.

The PBA is established and maintained by the *Purchaser*. Amounts due to the *Supplier* are paid into the Project Bank by the *Purchaser* and his employer, and payment to the *Supplier* is made by the Project Bank.

The Trust Deed is intended to allow payment to the *Supplier* to continue in the event of the insolvency of the *Purchaser*. The deed is executed by the *Purchaser* and his employer, the *Supplier*, and other suppliers or sub-contractors to the *Purchaser*. The *Supplier* will sign the Trust Deed when he has been identified in the *Purchaser*'s contract with his employer, or sign the Joining Deed if added later.

1: Project Bank Account

Definitions	1.1	(1) Project Bank Account is the account established by the *Purchaser* and used to make payments to the *Supplier*.

(2) Trust Deed is an agreement in the form set out in the contract which contains provisions for administering the Project Bank Account.

(3) Joining Deed is an agreement in the form set out in the contract under which the *Supplier* joins the Trust Deed. |
Payments	1.2	The *Supplier* receives payment from the Project Bank Account of the amount due from the *Purchaser* as soon as practicable after the Project Bank Account receives payment.
	1.3	A payment which is due from the *Supplier* to the *Purchaser* is not made through the Project Bank Account.
Effect of payment	1.4	Payments made from the Project Bank Account are treated as payments from the *Purchaser* to the *Supplier* in accordance with this contract.

If the *Supplier* is identified as a Named Supplier in the Contract Data for the *Purchaser*'s contract with his employer

Trust Deed	1.5	The *Purchaser*, his employer and the *Supplier* sign the Trust Deed before the first assessment date in the contract between the *Contractor* and his employer.

If the *Supplier* is added as a Named Supplier after the *Purchaser*'s contract with his employer came into existence

Trust Deed	1.5	The *Purchaser*, his employer and the *Supplier* sign the Joining Deed before the first *assessment day*.
Termination	1.6	If the *Purchaser* issues a termination certificate, no further payment is made into the Project Bank Account.

Trust Deed

This agreement is made between the *Employer,* the *Contractor* and the Named Suppliers.

Terms in this deed have the meanings given to them in the contract between .... and .... for .... (the *works*).

Background

The *Employer* and the *Contractor* have entered into a contract for the *works.*

The Named Suppliers have entered into contracts with the *Contractor* or a Subcontractor in connection with the *works.*

The *Contractor* has established a Project Bank Account to make provision for payment to the *Contractor* and the Named Suppliers.

Agreement

The parties to this deed agree that

- sums due to the *Contractor* and Named Suppliers and set out in the Authorisation are held in trust in the Project Bank Account by the *Contractor* for distribution to the *Contractor* and Named Suppliers in accordance with the banking arrangements applicable to the Project Bank Account,
- further Named Suppliers may be added as parties to this deed with the agreement of the *Employer* and *Contractor.* The agreement of the *Employer* and *Contractor* is treated as agreement by the Named Suppliers who are parties to this deed,
- this deed is subject to the law of the contract for the *works,*
- the benefits under this deed may not be assigned.

Executed as a deed on ....

by

.... (*Employer*)

.... (*Contractor*)

....

....

....

....

(Named Suppliers)

Joining Deed

This agreement is made between the *Employer,* the *Contractor* and .... (the Additional Supplier).

Terms in this deed have the meanings given to them in the contract between .... and .... for .... (the *works*).

Background

The *Employer* and the *Contractor* have entered into a contract for the *works*.

The Named Suppliers have entered into contracts with the *Contractor* or a Subcontractor in connection with the *works*.

The *Contractor* has established a Project Bank Account to make provision for payment to the *Contractor* and the Named Suppliers.

The *Employer,* the *Contractor* and the Named Suppliers have entered into a deed as set out in Annex 1 (the Trust Deed), and have agreed that the Additional Supplier may join that deed.

Agreement

The Parties to this deed agree that

- the Additional Supplier becomes a party to the Trust Deed from the date set out below,

- this deed is subject to the law of the contract for the *works*,

- the benefits under this deed may not be assigned.

Executed as a deed on ....

by

.... (*Employer*)

.... (*Contractor*)

.... (Additional Supplier)

Stage A How a *Purchaser* invites tenders for goods

Example A1 Title page

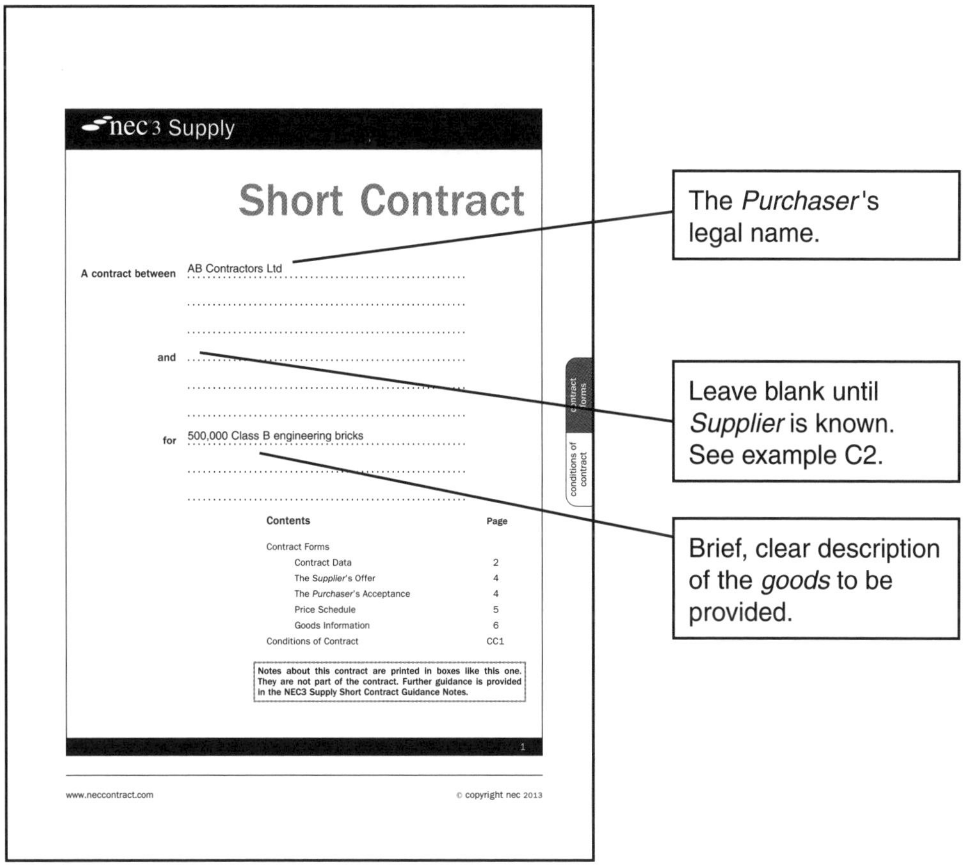

nec3 Supply

Short Contract

A contract between AB Contractors Ltd

and

for 500,000 Class B engineering bricks

Contents | Page

Notes about this contract are printed in boxes like this one. They are not part of the contract. Further guidance is provided in the NEC3 Supply Short Contract Guidance Notes.

contract forms | conditions of contract

1

www.neccontract.com © copyright nec 2013

Example A2   Contract Data

Description of the *goods* to be provided (as on title page).

GN on clause 13.2.

GN on clause 30.1.

GN on clause 42.2.

GN on clause 41.1.

GN on clause 50.1.

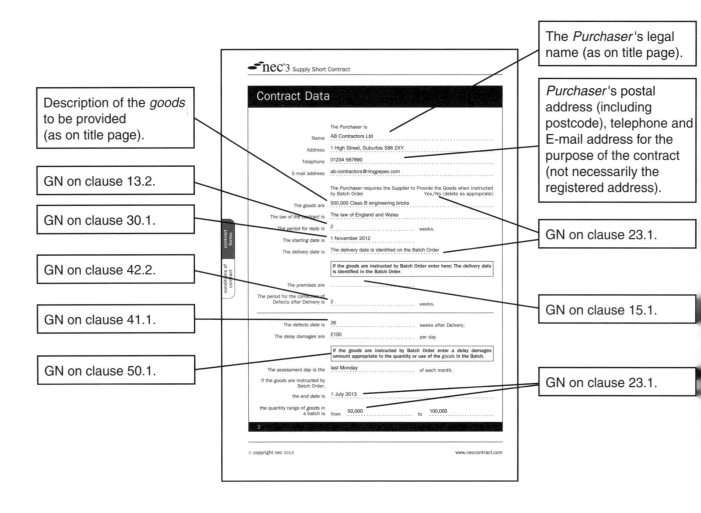

The *Purchaser*'s legal name (as on title page).

Purchaser's postal address (including postcode), telephone and E-mail address for the purpose of the contract (not necessarily the registered address).

GN on clause 23.1.

GN on clause 15.1.

GN on clause 23.1.

GN on clause 51.2.

GN on clause 86.2.

State any insurances which the *Purchaser* will provide which are included in the contract. GN on clause 84.1.

State name, postal address with postcode, telephone and E-mail address of the *Adjudicator*. GN on clause 93.2.

GN on clause 86.1.

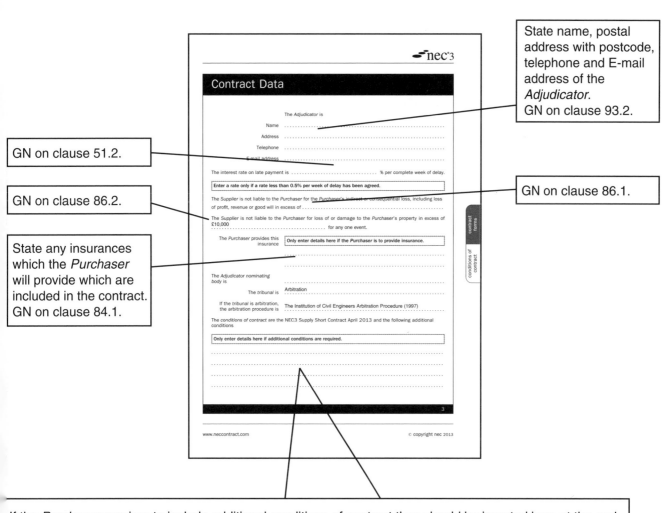

Contract Data

The *Adjudicator* is

Name ....

Address ....

Telephone ....

E-mail address ....

The interest rate on late payment is .... % per complete week of delay.

Enter a rate only if a rate less than 0.5% per week of delay has been agreed.

The *Supplier* is not liable to the *Purchaser* for the *Purchaser's* indirect or consequential loss, including loss of profit, revenue or good will in excess of ....

The *Supplier* is not liable to the *Purchaser* for loss of or damage to the *Purchaser's* property in excess of £10,000 .... for any one event.

The *Purchaser* provides this insurance | Only enter details here if the *Purchaser* is to provide insurance.

The *Adjudicator* nominating body is

The *tribunal* is   Arbitration

If the *tribunal* is arbitration, the arbitration procedure is   The Institution of Civil Engineers Arbitration Procedure (1997)

The *conditions of contract* are the NEC3 Supply Short Contract April 2013 and the following additional conditions

Only enter details here if additional conditions are required.

3

www.neccontract.com   © copyright nec 2013

If the *Purchaser* requires to include additional conditions of contract they should be inserted here at the end of the Contract Data. Any additional conditions should be drafted in the same style as the SSC clauses, using the same defined terms and other terminology. They should be carefully checked, preferably by flowcharting, to ensure that they mesh with the SSC clauses.

Additional conditions should be used only when absolutely necessary to accommodate special needs which are not covered by the SSC clauses. See notes on additional compensation events under clause 60.1.

Many special needs can be accommodated during the tender by instructions in the Goods Information.

Stage B   How a tenderer makes an offer

Example B1   The *Supplier*'s Offer

The tenderer's legal name.

Tenderer's postal address (including postcode), telephone and E-mail address for the purpose of the contract.

Enter the percentage to be added to payments. GNs on clauses 11.2(2) and 63.2.

Offer to be signed by a person in the tenderer's organisation having the necessary authority.

Left blank until completed at a later stage by the *Purchaser*. See example C1.

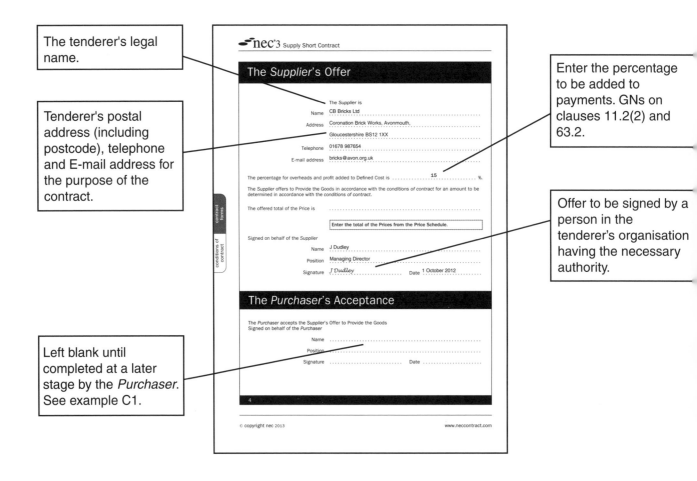

nec°3 Supply Short Contract

The *Supplier*'s Offer

The *Supplier* is

Name CB Bricks Ltd

Address Coronation Brick Works, Avonmouth,

Gloucestershire BS12 1XX

Telephone 01678 987654

E-mail address bricks@avon.org.uk

The percentage for overheads and profit added to Defined Cost is .... **15** .... %.

The *Supplier* offers to Provide the Goods in accordance with the *conditions of contract* for an amount to be determined in accordance with the *conditions of contract*.

The offered total of the Price is

| Enter the total of the Prices from the Price Schedule. |

Signed on behalf of the *Supplier*

Name J Dudley

Position Managing Director

Signature *J Dudley*   Date 1 October 2012

The *Purchaser*'s Acceptance

The *Purchaser* accepts the *Supplier*'s Offer to Provide the Goods
Signed on behalf of the *Purchaser*

Name ....

Position ....

Signature .... Date ....

4

© copyright nec 2013   www.neccontract.com

Stage C   How a contract is made

Example C1   The *Purchaser*'s acceptance

Acceptance to be signed by a person having the necessary authority in the *Purchaser*'s organisation.

Example C2   Title page

Batch Order

Batch Order for Contract ref. . . . .

Batch Order No. . . . .

To . . . . (*Supplier*)

I instruct you to supply the following *goods*

Item number	Description	Unit	Quantity	Rate	Price
	The total of the Prices of the Batch Order				

The start date is . . . .

The *delivery date* is . . . .

Signed . . . . (for *Purchaser*)

Flow charts for the

Supply Short Contract

FLOW CHARTS

PREFACE

These flow charts depict the procedures followed when using the NEC3 Supply Short Contract (SSC). They are intended to help people using the SSC to see how the various SSC clauses produce clear and precise sequences of action for the people involved.

The flow charts are not part of any contract. Much of the text and many of the words taken from the SSC itself are abbreviated in the flow charts. The flow charts depict almost all of the sequences of action set out in the SSC. Many of the sequences interact, and because of this, users of the flow charts will often have to review more than one sheet in order to track the full sequence of actions in one area.

ABBREVIATIONS USED IN THE FLOW CHART BOXES

FC 16	Flow chart for clause 16
CD	Contract Data
CE	Compensation event
GI	Goods Information
P	Purchaser
P&M	Plant and Materials
S	Supplier
SC	Subcontractor

ABBREVIATIONS USED IN THE FLOW CHART BOXES

Legend

CHART START

HEADINGS
 Headings in caps
 provide guidance

STATEMENTS
 If a sub clause is
 referenced, text
 is from the NEC

LOGIC LINKS
 Links go to right
 and/or downward
 unless shown

QUESTION
 Answer question
 to determine the
 route to follow

SUBROUTINE
 Include another
 flow chart here

CONTINUATION
 Link to matching
 point(s) on other
 chart sheets

CHART TITLE
 Chart number,
 title and sheet

CONTINUATION

CHART FINISH

CHART TITLE

Start

HELPFUL HEADING

Statement
explaining
next step

Sub clause or
Statement using part or all of the NEC
text in subclause

Does
this sub clause
apply?

YES

NO

FC or
Description

A
sheet 2

B
sheet 2

Flow chart or Sheet 1 of 2
Description

A
sheet 2

B
sheet 2

Finish

Flow chart or Sheet 2 of 2
Description

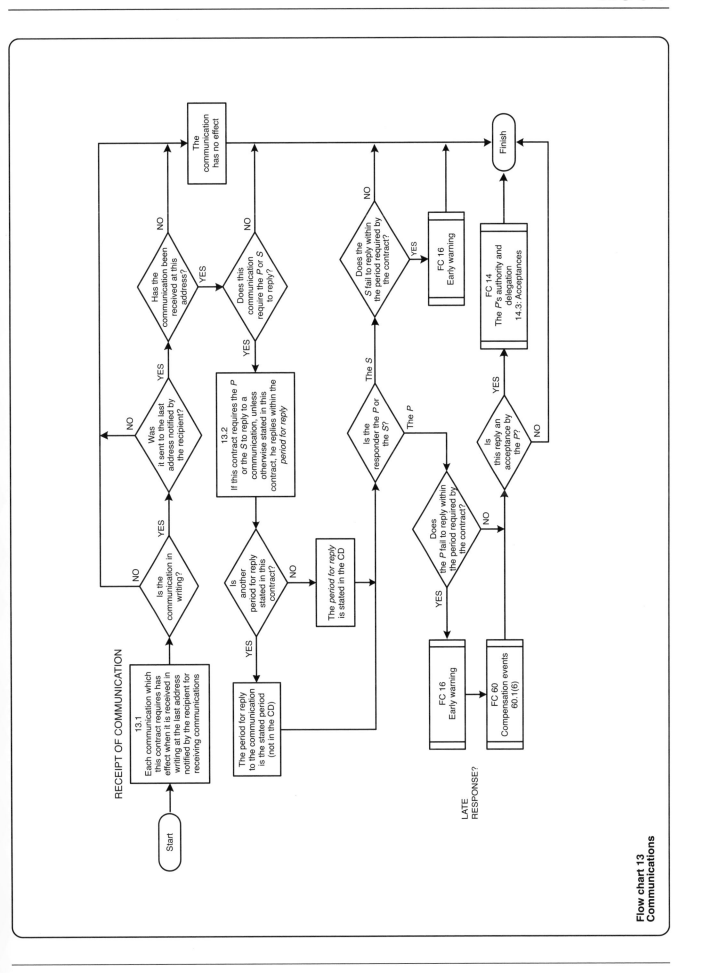

RECEIPT OF COMMUNICATION

13.1
Each communication which this contract requires has effect when it is received in writing at the last address notified by the recipient for receiving communications

13.2
If this contract requires the *P* or the *S* to reply to a communication, unless otherwise stated in this contract, he replies within the *period for reply*

Is the communication in writing?

Was it sent to the last address notified by the recipient?

Has the communication been received at this address?

The communication has no effect

Does this communication require the *P* or *S* to reply?

Is another period for reply stated in this contract?

The period for reply to the communication is the stated period (not in the CD)

The *period for reply* is stated in the CD

Is the responder the *P* or the *S*?

The *S*

The *P*

Does the *S* fail to reply within the period required by the contract?

FC 16
Early warning

Does the *P* fail to reply within the period required by the contract?

FC 16
Early warning

FC 60
Compensation events
60.1(6)

Is this reply an acceptance by the *P*?

FC 14
The *P*'s authority and delegation
14.3: Acceptances

Finish

LATE RESPONSE?

Start

**Flow chart 13
Communications**

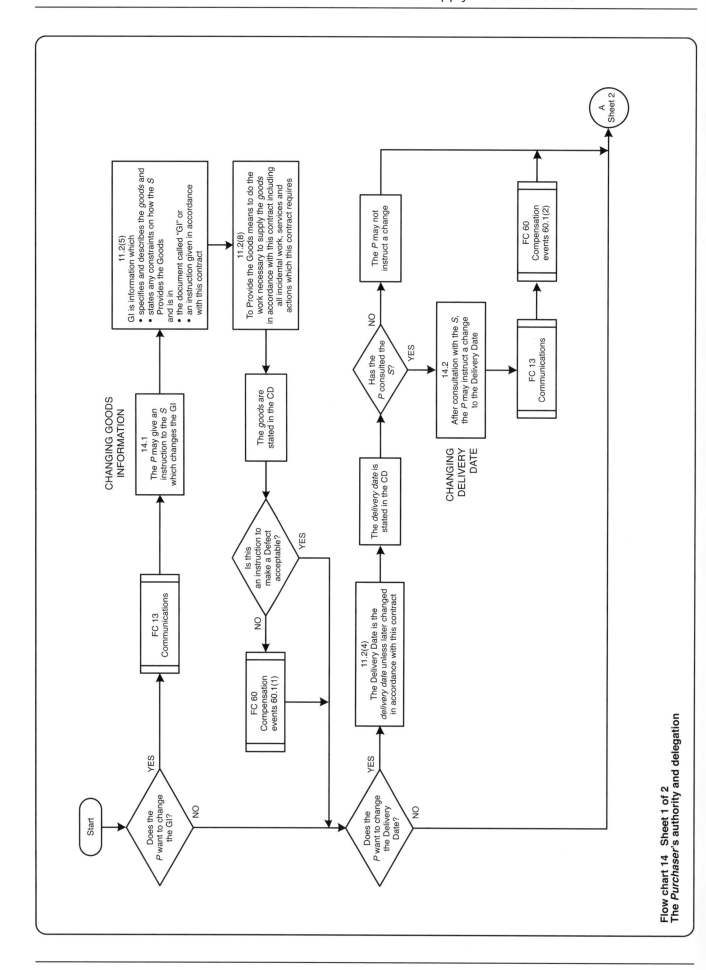

CHANGING GOODS INFORMATION

Start

Does the P want to change the GI? — YES →

FC 13 Communications

14.1 The P may give an instruction to the S which changes the GI

11.2(5) GI is information which
• specifies and describes the goods and states any constraints on how the S Provides the Goods
and is in
• the document called "GI" or
• an instruction given in accordance with this contract

11.2(8) To Provide the Goods means to do the work necessary to supply the goods in accordance with this contract including all incidental work, services and actions which this contract requires

The goods are stated in the CD

Is this an instruction to make a Defect acceptable? — NO →

FC 60 Compensation events 60.1(1)

YES →

Does the P want to change the Delivery Date? — NO →

YES →

11.2(4) The Delivery Date is the delivery date unless later changed in accordance with this contract

The delivery date is stated in the CD

Has the P consulted the S? — NO →

The P may not instruct a change

YES →

CHANGING DELIVERY DATE

14.2 After consultation with the S, the P may instruct a change to the Delivery Date

FC 13 Communications

FC 60 Compensation events 60.1(2)

A Sheet 2

Flow chart 14   Sheet 1 of 2
The Purchaser's authority and delegation

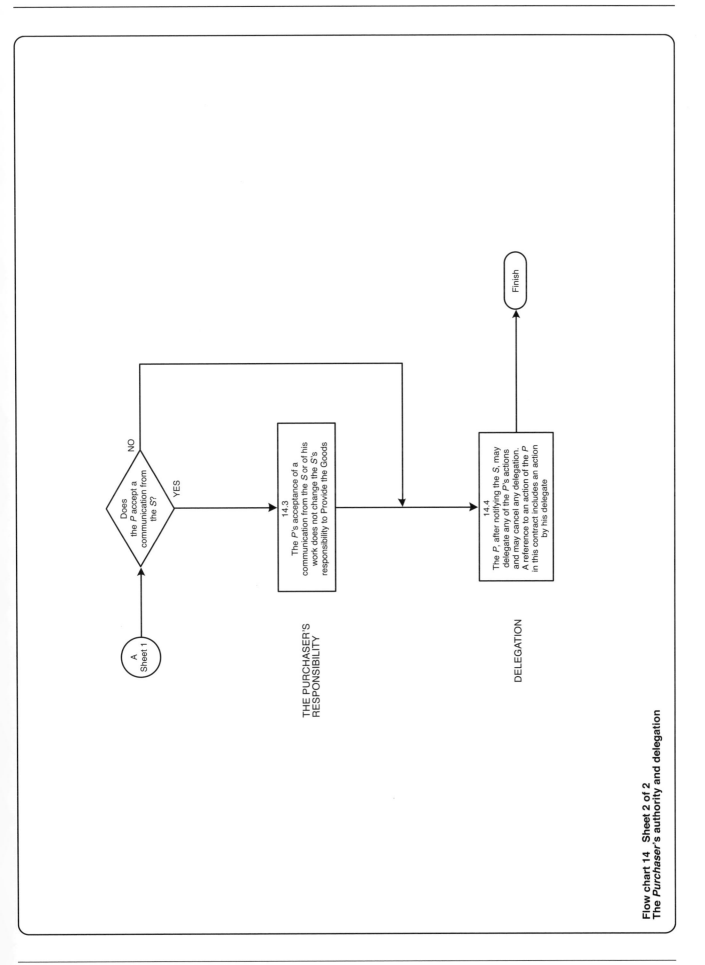

Does the P accept a communication from the S?

NO

YES

A
Sheet 1

14.3
The P's acceptance of a communication from the S or of his work does not change the S's responsibility to Provide the Goods

THE PURCHASER'S RESPONSIBILITY

14.4
The P, after notifying the S, may delegate any of the P's actions and may cancel any delegation. A reference to an action of the P in this contract includes an action by his delegate

DELEGATION

Finish

Flow chart 14   Sheet 2 of 2
The *Purchaser's* authority and delegation

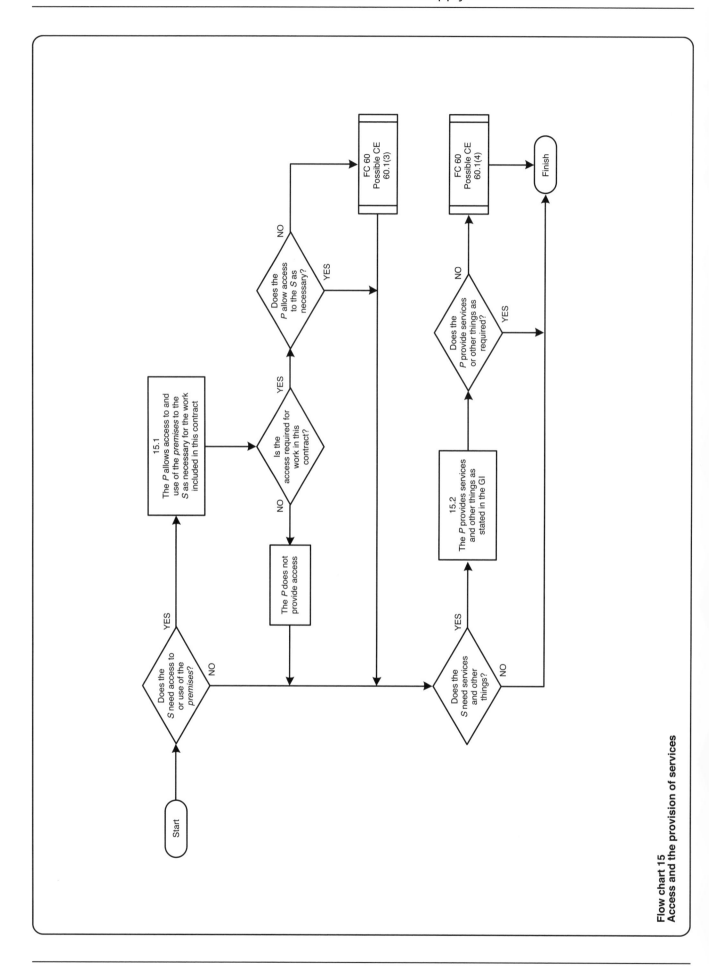

Flow chart 15
Access and the provision of services

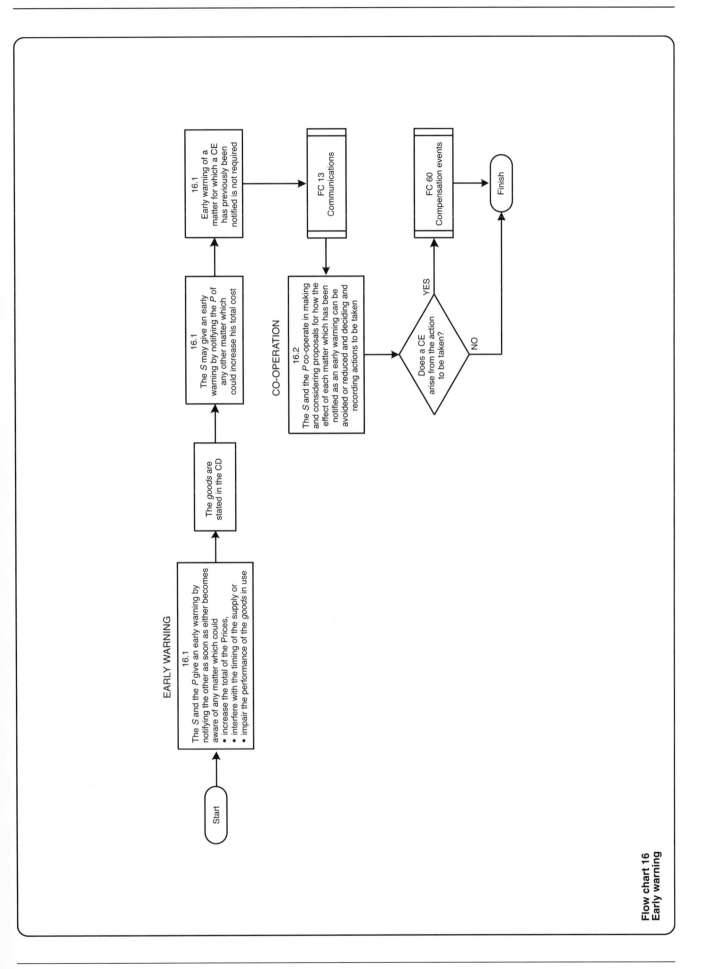

EARLY WARNING

16.1
The S and the P give an early warning by notifying the other as soon as either becomes aware of any matter which could
• increase the total of the Prices,
• interfere with the timing of the supply or
• impair the performance of the *goods* in use

The *goods* are stated in the CD

16.1
The S may give an early warning by notifying the P of any other matter which could increase his total cost

16.1
Early warning of a matter for which a CE has previously been notified is not required

Start

CO-OPERATION

16.2
The S and the P co-operate in making and considering proposals for how the effect of each matter which has been notified as an early warning can be avoided or reduced and deciding and recording actions to be taken

FC 13
Communications

FC 60
Compensation events

Does a CE arise from the action to be taken?

YES

NO

Finish

**Flow chart 16
Early warning**

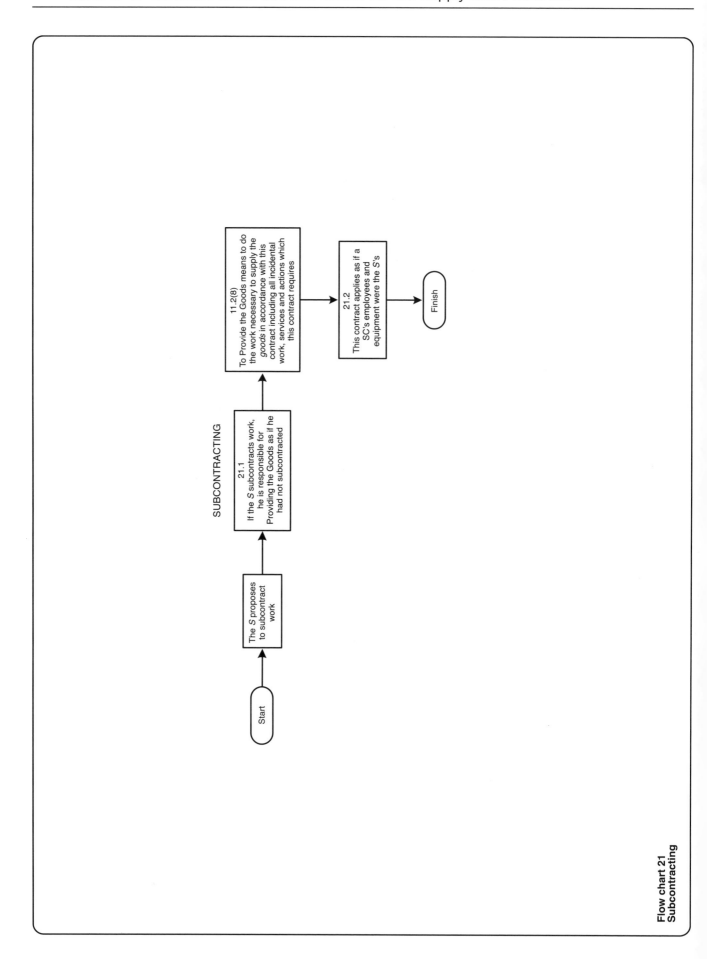

SUBCONTRACTING

Start

The *S* proposes to subcontract work

21.1
If the *S* subcontracts work, he is responsible for Providing the Goods as if he had not subcontracted

11.2(8)
To Provide the Goods means to do the work necessary to supply the *goods* in accordance with this contract including all incidental work, services and actions which this contract requires

21.2
This contract applies as if a SC's employees and equipment were the *S*'s

Finish

**Flow chart 21
Subcontracting**

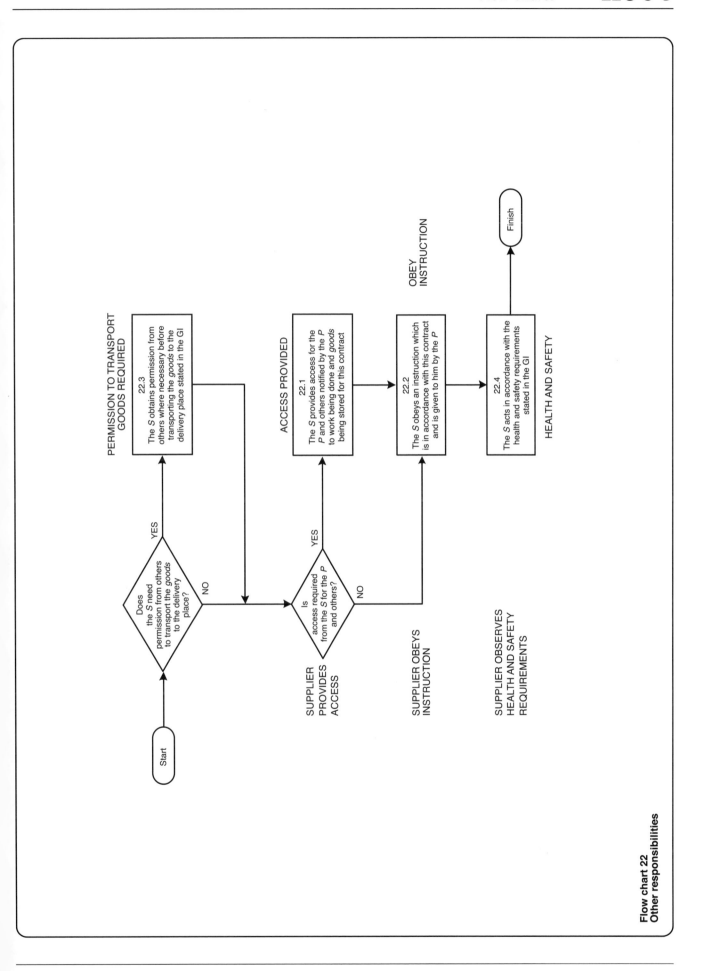

PERMISSION TO TRANSPORT
GOODS REQUIRED

22.3
The S obtains permission from
others where necessary before
transporting the goods to the
delivery place stated in the GI

ACCESS PROVIDED

22.1
The S provides access for the
P and others notified by the P
to work being done and goods
being stored for this contract

OBEY
INSTRUCTION

22.2
The S obeys an instruction which
is in accordance with this contract
and is given to him by the P

Finish

HEALTH AND SAFETY

22.4
The S acts in accordance with the
health and safety requirements
stated in the GI

Start

Does
the S need
permission from others
to transport the goods
to the delivery
place?

YES

NO

Is
access required
from the S for the P
and others?

YES

NO

SUPPLIER
PROVIDES
ACCESS

SUPPLIER OBEYS
INSTRUCTION

SUPPLIER OBSERVES
HEALTH AND SAFETY
REQUIREMENTS

Flow chart 22
Other responsibilities

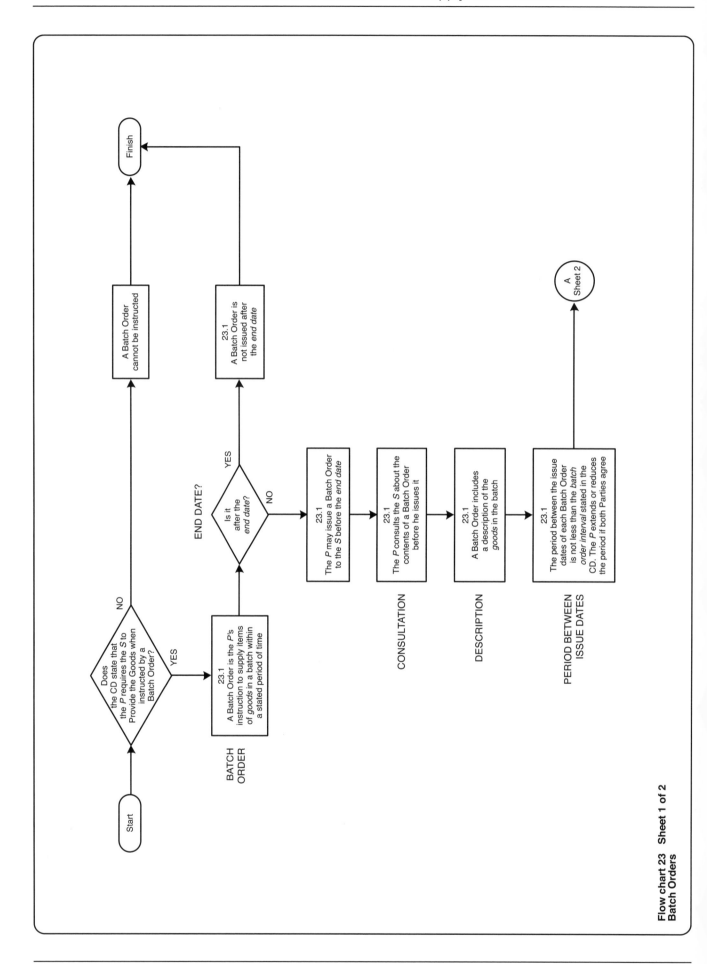

Flow chart 23   Sheet 1 of 2
Batch Orders

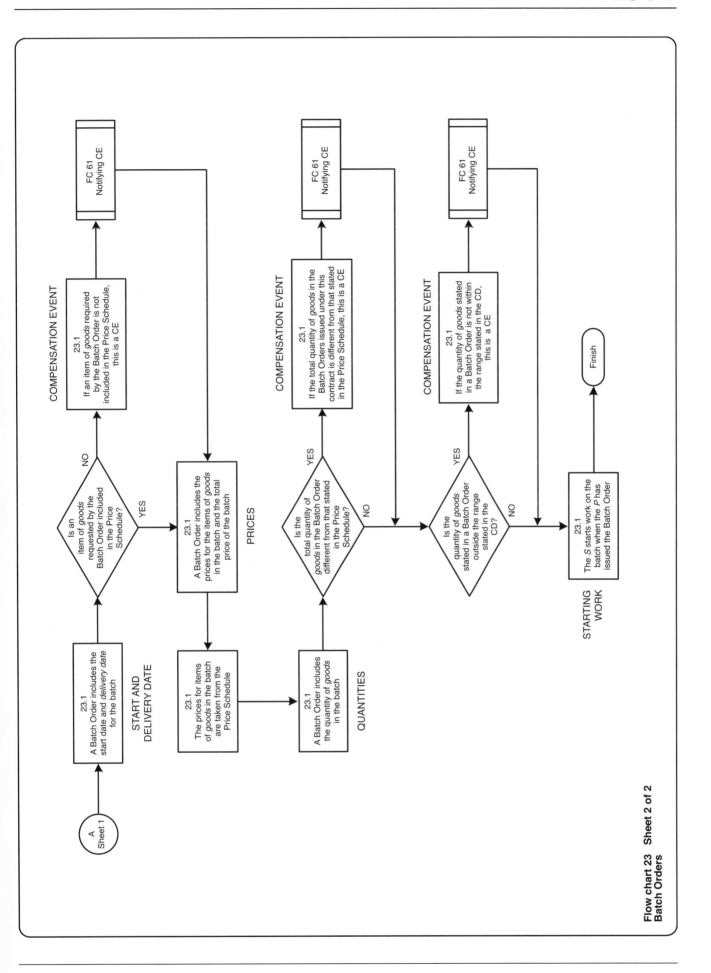

COMPENSATION EVENT

23.1
If an item of *goods* required by the Batch Order is not included in the Price Schedule, this is a CE

FC 61
Notifying CE

Is an item of *goods* requested by the Batch Order included in the Price Schedule?

NO

YES

23.1
A Batch Order includes the prices for the items of *goods* in the batch and the total price of the batch

PRICES

23.1
A Batch Order includes the start date and *delivery date* for the batch

START AND DELIVERY DATE

A
Sheet 1

23.1
The prices for items of *goods* in the batch are taken from the Price Schedule

23.1
A Batch Order includes the quantity of *goods* in the batch

QUANTITIES

COMPENSATION EVENT

23.1
If the total quantity of *goods* in the Batch Orders issued under this contract is different from that stated in the Price Schedule, this is a CE

FC 61
Notifying CE

Is the total quantity of *goods* in the Batch Order different from that stated in the Price Schedule?

YES

NO

COMPENSATION EVENT

23.1
If the quantity of *goods* stated in a Batch Order is not within the range stated in the CD, this is a CE

FC 61
Notifying CE

Is the quantity of *goods* stated in a Batch Order outside the range stated in the CD?

YES

NO

23.1
The *S* starts work on the batch when the *P* has issued the Batch Order

STARTING WORK

Finish

Flow chart 23   Sheet 2 of 2
Batch Orders

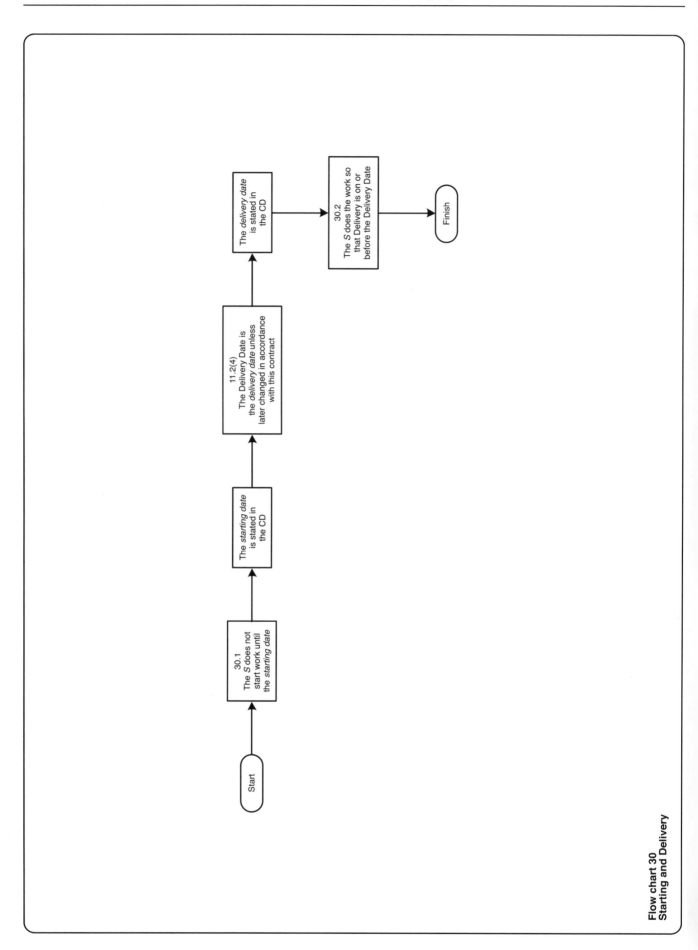

Start

30.1
The S does not
start work until
the *starting date*

The *starting date*
is stated in
the CD

11.2(4)
The Delivery Date is
the *delivery date* unless
later changed in accordance
with this contract

The *delivery date*
is stated in
the CD

30.2
The S does the work so
that Delivery is on or
before the Delivery Date

Finish

Flow chart 30
Starting and Delivery

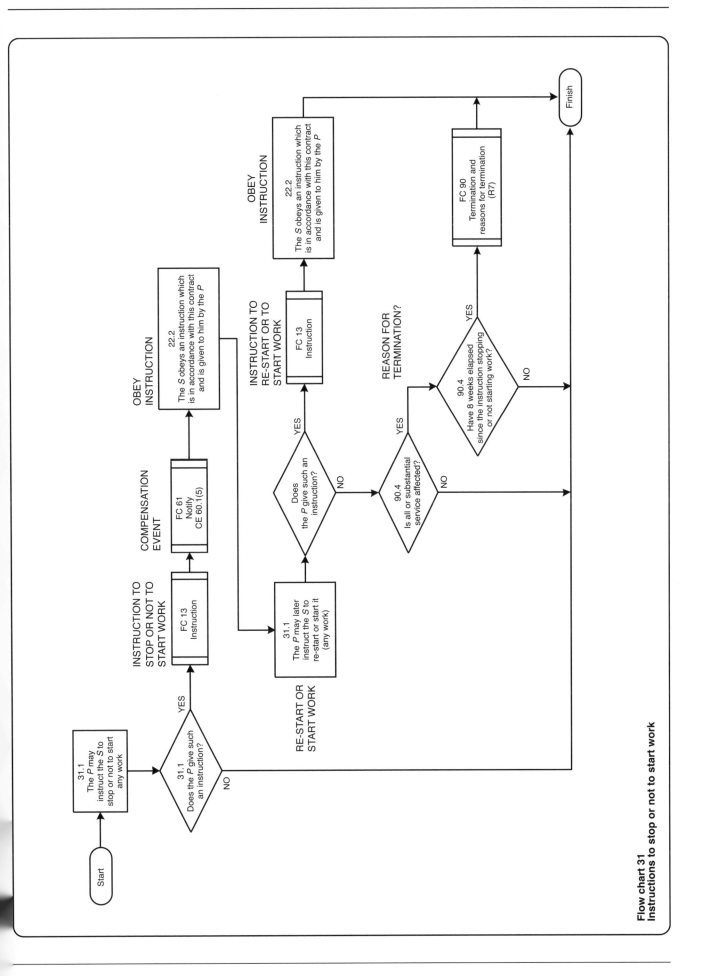

Flow chart 31
Instructions to stop or not to start work

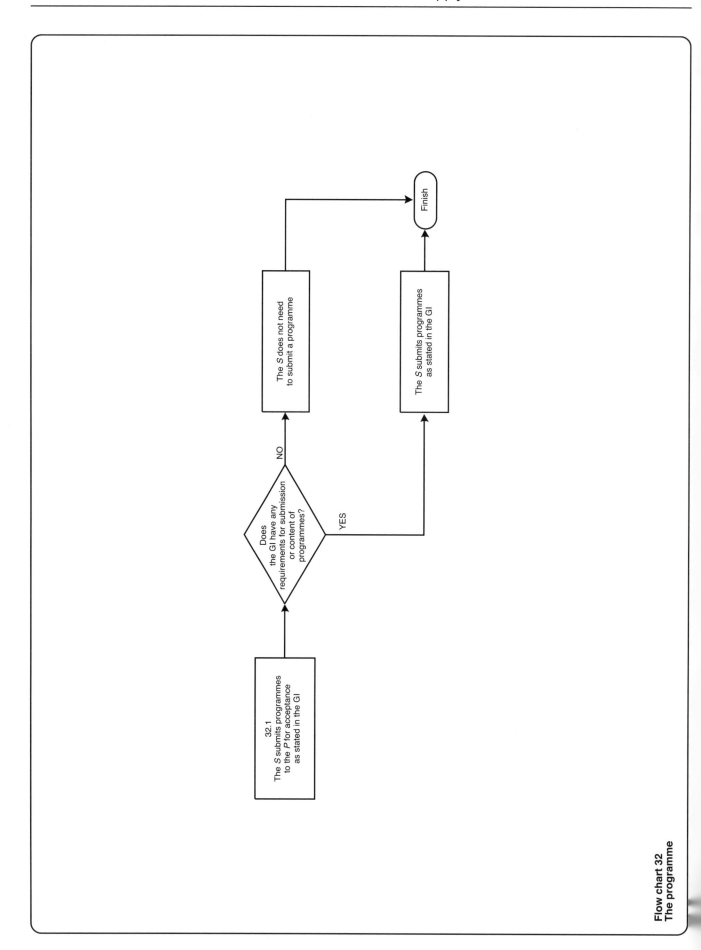

Flow chart 32
The programme

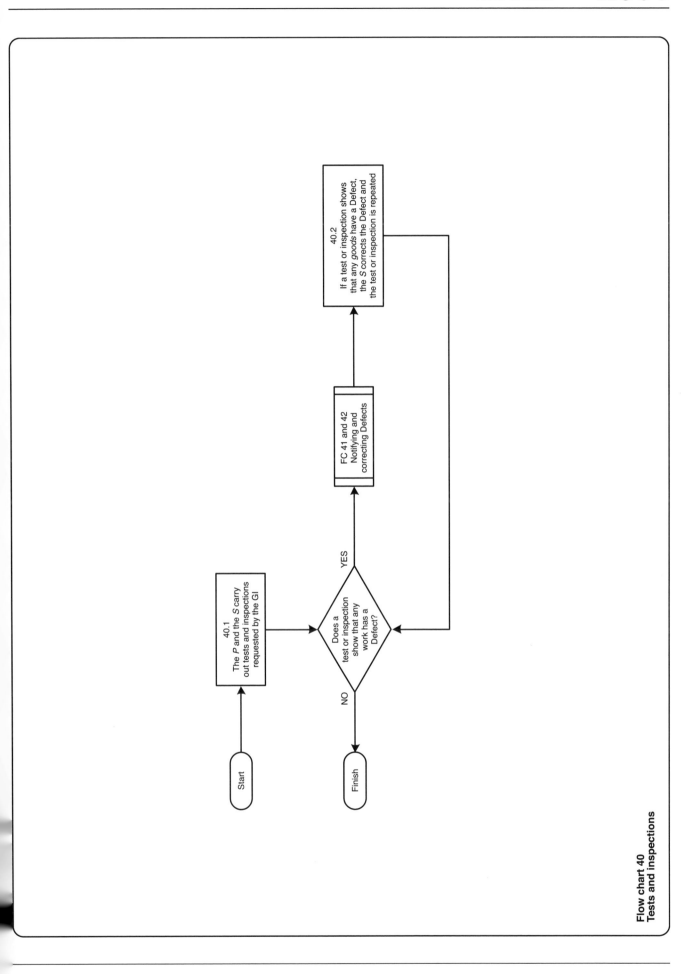

Flow chart 40
Tests and inspections

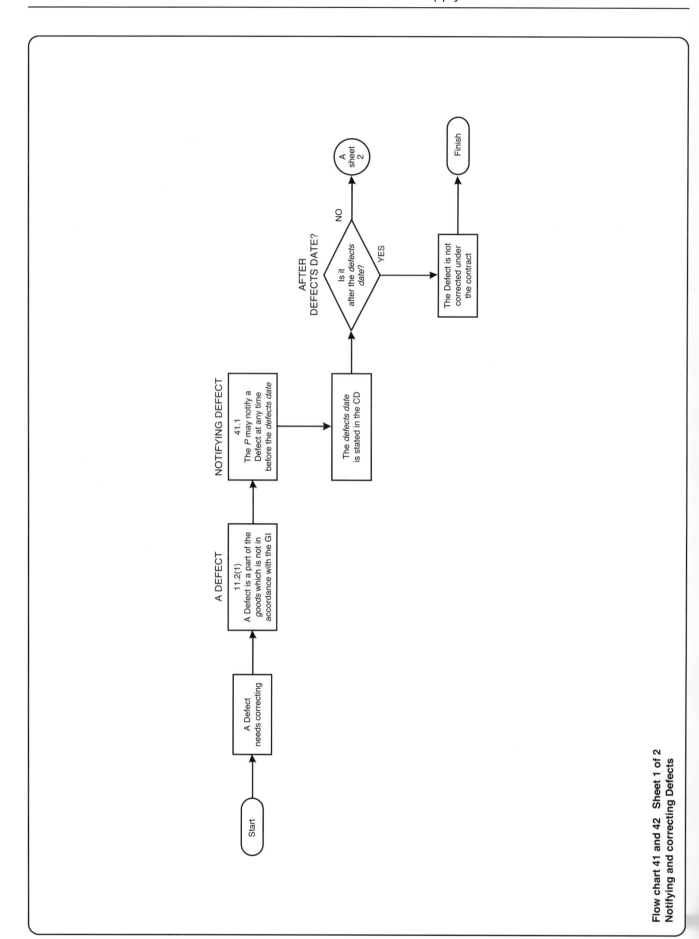

A DEFECT

NOTIFYING DEFECT

AFTER DEFECTS DATE?

Start

A Defect needs correcting

11.2(1)
A Defect is a part of the *goods* which is not in accordance with the GI

41.1
The *P* may notify a Defect at any time before the *defects date*

The *defects date* is stated in the CD

Is it after the *defects date*?

NO → A sheet 2

YES → The Defect is not corrected under the contract → Finish

Flow chart 41 and 42   Sheet 1 of 2
Notifying and correcting Defects

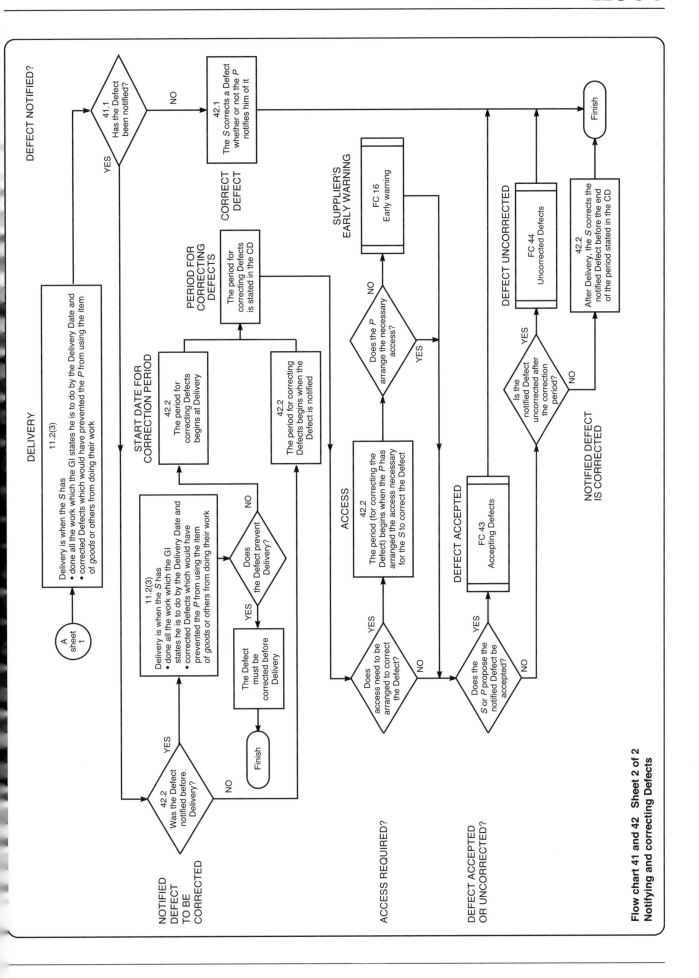

Flow chart 41 and 42   Sheet 2 of 2
Notifying and correcting Defects

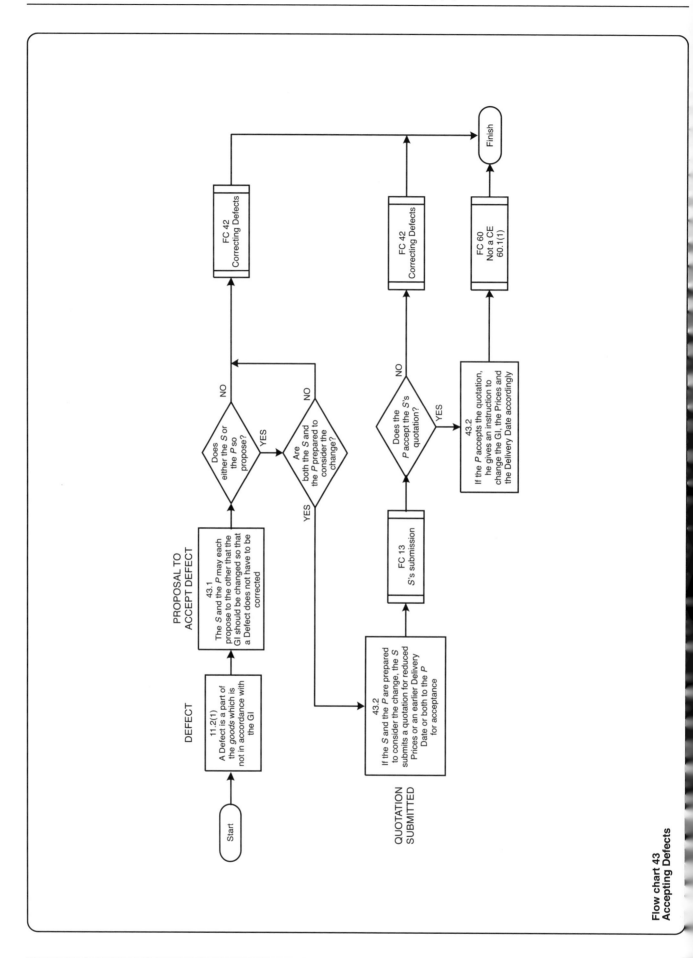

Flow chart 43
Accepting Defects

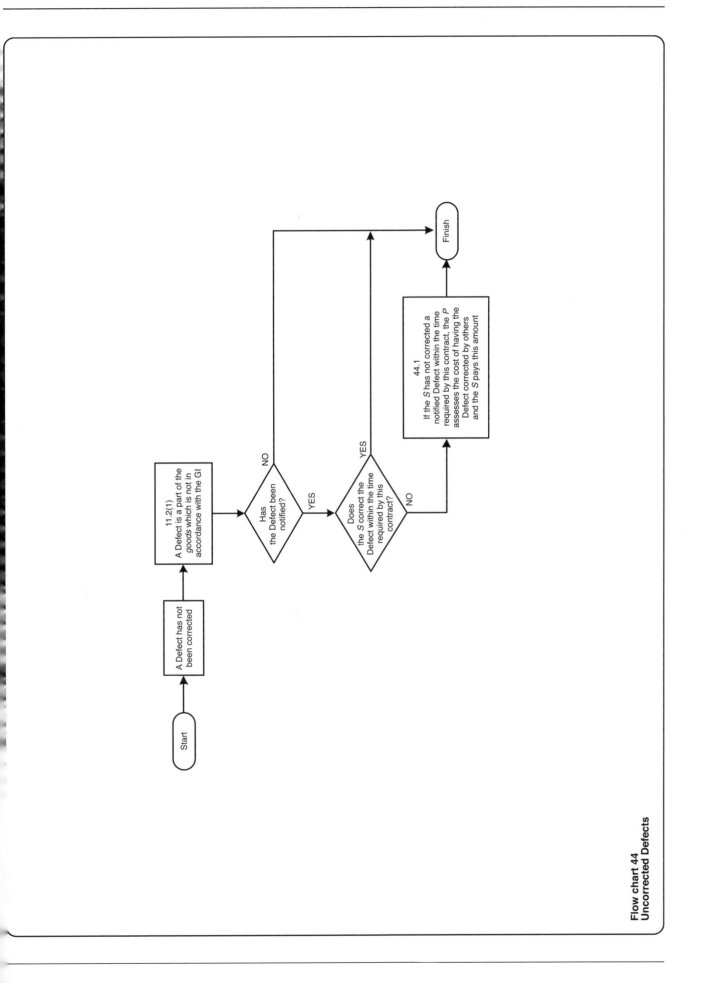

Flow chart 44
Uncorrected Defects

Start

A Defect has not
been corrected

11.2(1)
A Defect is a part of the
goods which is not in
accordance with the GI

Has
the Defect been
notified?

NO

YES

Does
the *S* correct the
Defect within the time
required by this
contract?

YES

NO

44.1
If the *S* has not corrected a
notified Defect within the time
required by this contract, the *P*
assesses the cost of having the
Defect corrected by others
and the *S* pays this amount

Finish

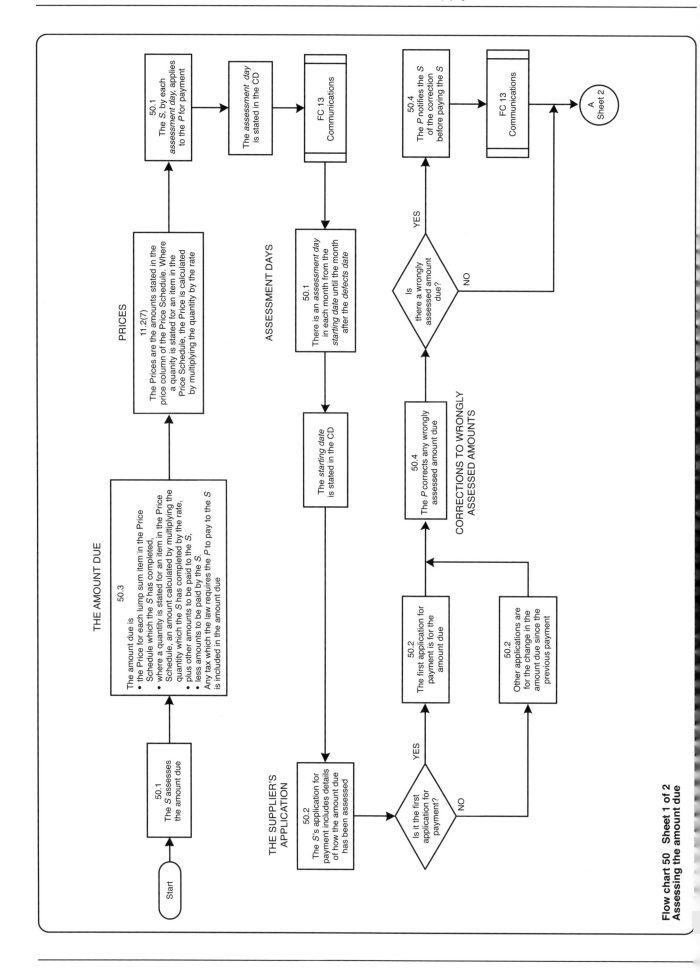

THE AMOUNT DUE

Start

50.1
The S assesses the amount due

50.3
The amount due is
• the Price for each lump sum item in the Price Schedule which the S has completed,
• where a quantity is stated for an item in the Price Schedule, an amount calculated by multiplying the quantity which the S has completed by the rate,
• plus other amounts to be paid to the S,
• less amounts to be paid by the S.
Any tax which the law requires the P to pay to the S is included in the amount due

PRICES

11.2(7)
The Prices are the amounts stated in the price column of the Price Schedule. Where a quantity is stated for an item in the Price Schedule, the Price is calculated by multiplying the quantity by the rate

50.1
The S, by each assessment day, applies to the P for payment

The assessment day is stated in the CD

FC 13
Communications

ASSESSMENT DAYS

50.1
There is an assessment day in each month from the starting date until the month after the defects date

The starting date is stated in the CD

THE SUPPLIER'S APPLICATION

50.2
The S's application for payment includes details of how the amount due has been assessed

Is it the first application for payment?

— YES → 50.2 The first application for payment is for the amount due

— NO → 50.2 Other applications are for the change in the amount due since the previous payment

CORRECTIONS TO WRONGLY ASSESSED AMOUNTS

50.4
The P corrects any wrongly assessed amount due

Is there a wrongly assessed amount due?

— YES → 50.4 The P notifies the S of the correction before paying the S

FC 13
Communications

— NO →

A
Sheet 2

**Flow chart 50   Sheet 1 of 2
Assessing the amount due**

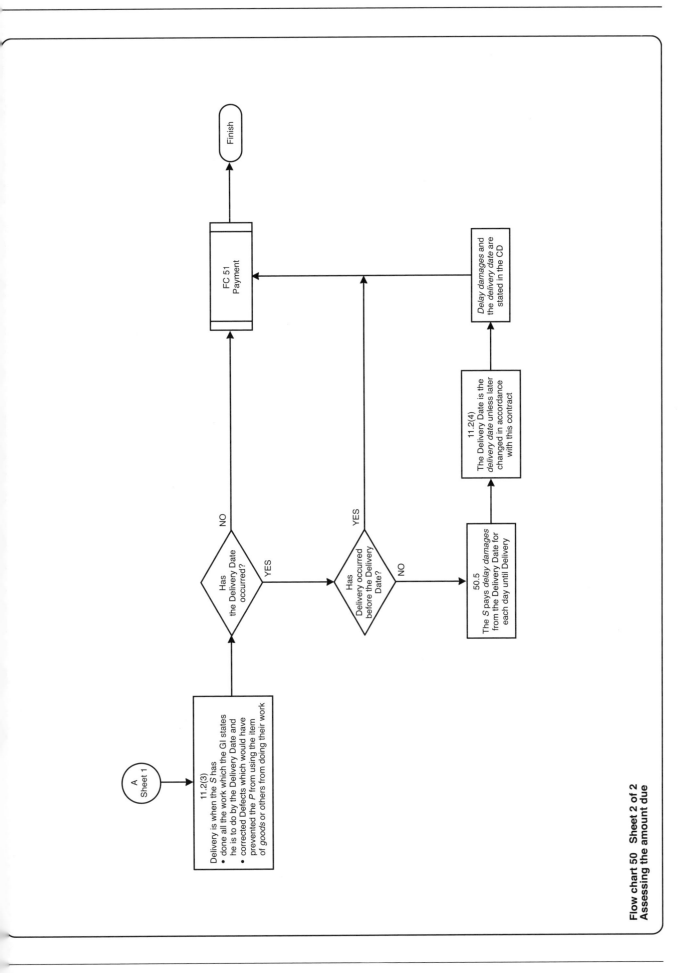

FC 51
Payment

Delay damages and
the *delivery date* are
stated in the CD

NO

11.2(4)
The Delivery Date is the
delivery date unless later
changed in accordance
with this contract

Has
the Delivery Date
occurred?

YES

Has
Delivery occurred
before the Delivery
Date?

YES

NO

50.5
The *S* pays *delay damages*
from the Delivery Date for
each day until Delivery

A
Sheet 1

11.2(3)
Delivery is when the *S* has
• done all the work which the GI states
  he is to do by the Delivery Date and
• corrected Defects which would have
  prevented the *P* from using the item
  of *goods* or others from doing their work

Flow chart 50 Sheet 2 of 2
Assessing the amount due

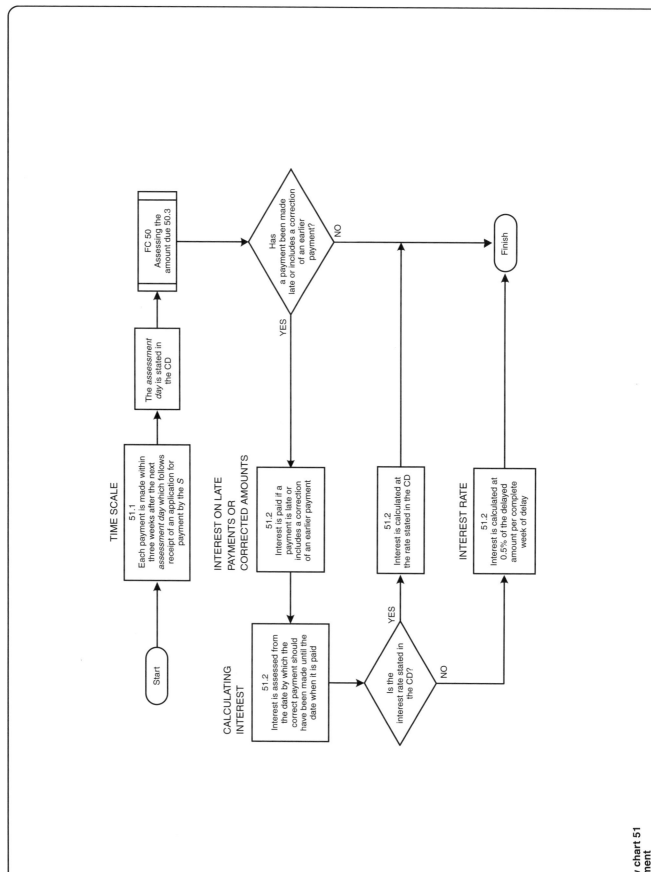

TIME SCALE

51.1
Each payment is made within three weeks after the next *assessment day* which follows receipt of an application for payment by the *S*

The *assessment day* is stated in the CD

FC 50
Assessing the amount due 50.3

INTEREST ON LATE PAYMENTS OR CORRECTED AMOUNTS

Has a payment been made late or includes a correction of an earlier payment?

51.2
Interest is paid if a payment is late or includes a correction of an earlier payment

CALCULATING INTEREST

51.2
Interest is assessed from the date by which the correct payment should have been made until the date when it is paid

Is the interest rate stated in the CD?

51.2
Interest is calculated at the rate stated in the CD

INTEREST RATE

51.2
Interest is calculated at 0.5% of the delayed amount per complete week of delay

Start

Finish

**Flow chart 51
Payment**

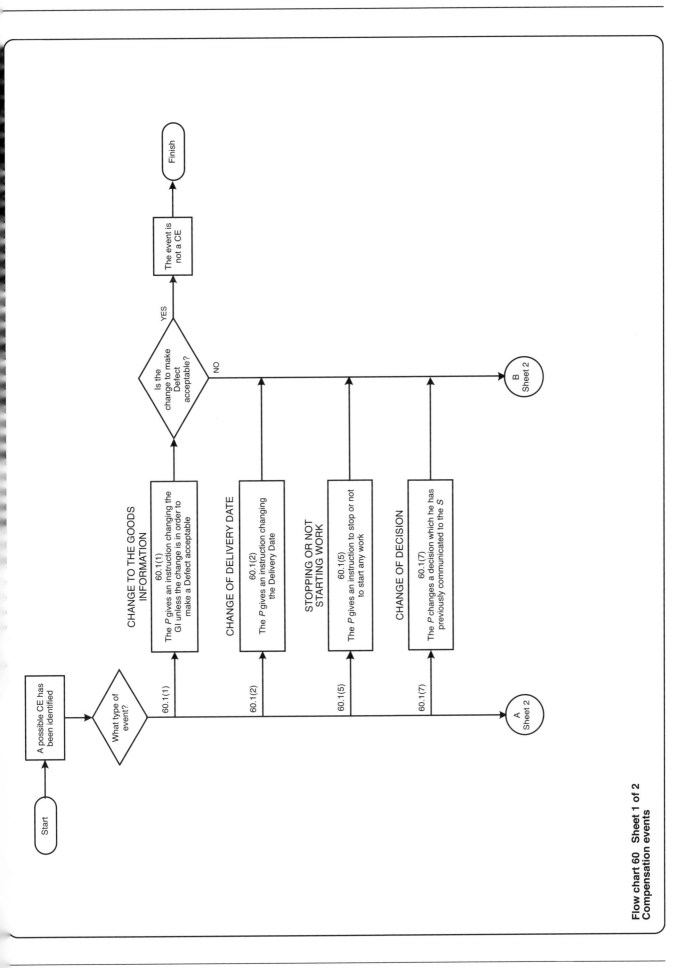

Flow chart 60 Sheet 1 of 2
Compensation events

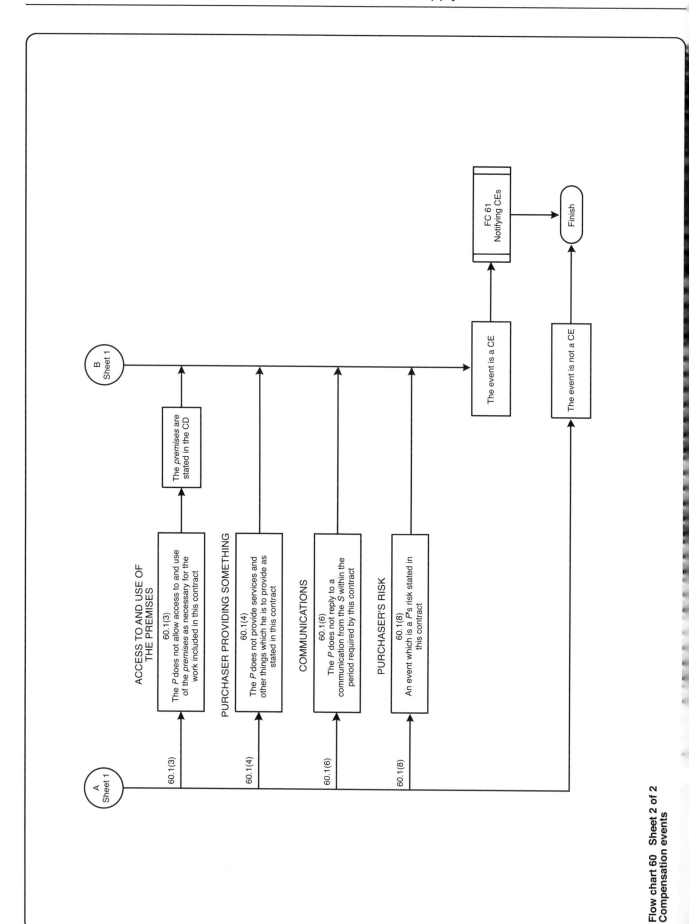

ACCESS TO AND USE OF THE PREMISES

60.1(3)
The *P* does not allow access to and use of the *premises* as necessary for the work included in this contract

The *premises* are stated in the CD

PURCHASER PROVIDING SOMETHING

60.1(4)
The *P* does not provide services and other things which he is to provide as stated in this contract

COMMUNICATIONS

60.1(6)
The *P* does not reply to a communication from the *S* within the period required by this contract

PURCHASER'S RISK

60.1(8)
An event which is a *P*'s risk stated in this contract

A Sheet 1

B Sheet 1

60.1(3)

60.1(4)

60.1(6)

60.1(8)

The event is a CE

The event is not a CE

FC 61 Notifying CEs

Finish

**Flow chart 60   Sheet 2 of 2
Compensation events**

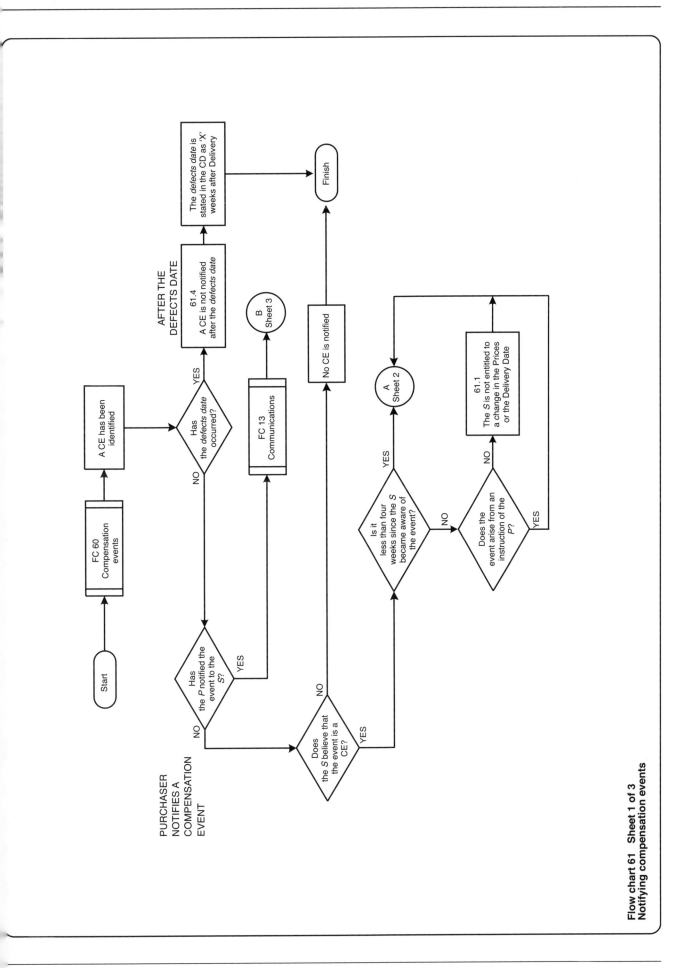

Flow chart 61   Sheet 1 of 3
Notifying compensation events

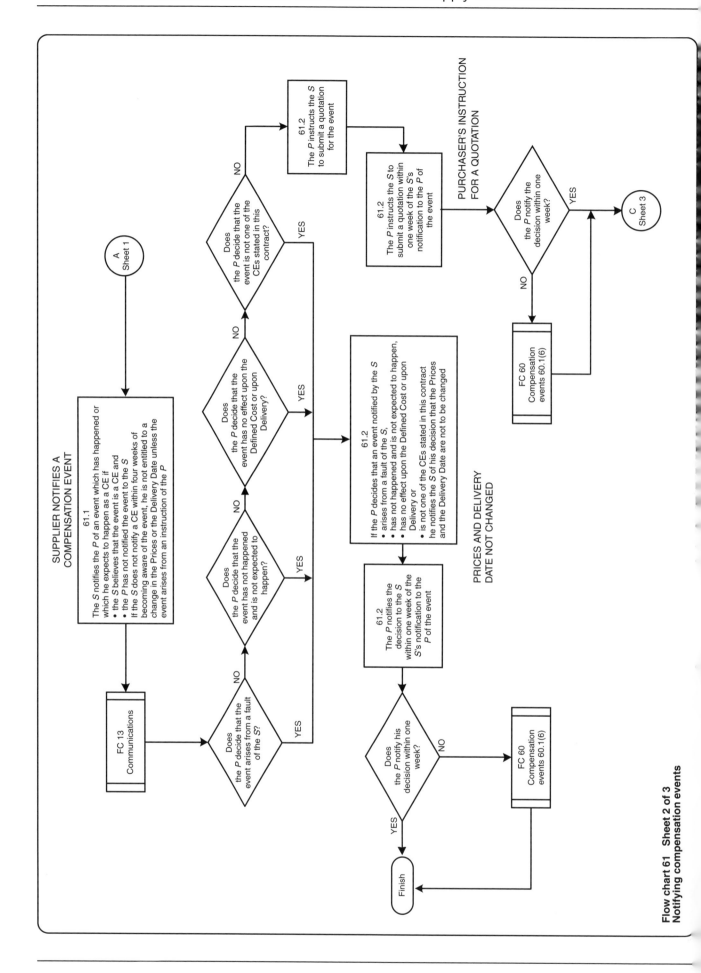

SUPPLIER NOTIFIES A COMPENSATION EVENT

61.1
The S notifies the P of an event which has happened or which he expects to happen as a CE if
• the S believes that the event is a CE and
• the P has not notified the event to the S
If the S does not notify a CE within four weeks of becoming aware of the event, he is not entitled to a change in the Prices or the Delivery Date unless the event arises from an instruction of the P

A Sheet 1

FC 13 Communications

Does the P decide that the event arises from a fault of the S?

Does the P decide that the event has not happened and is not expected to happen?

Does the P decide that the event has no effect upon the Defined Cost or upon Delivery?

Does the P decide that the event is not one of the CEs stated in this contract?

61.2
The P instructs the S to submit a quotation for the event

61.2
If the P decides that an event notified by the S
• arises from a fault of the S,
• has not happened and is not expected to happen,
• has no effect upon the Defined Cost or upon Delivery or
• is not one of the CEs stated in this contract
he notifies the S of his decision that the Prices and the Delivery Date are not to be changed

PRICES AND DELIVERY DATE NOT CHANGED

61.2
The P notifies the decision to the S within one week of the S's notification to the P of the event

Does the P notify his decision within one week?

FC 60 Compensation events 60.1(6)

Finish

61.2
The P instructs the S to submit a quotation within one week of the S's notification to the P of the event

PURCHASER'S INSTRUCTION FOR A QUOTATION

Does the P notify the decision within one week?

FC 60 Compensation events 60.1(6)

C Sheet 3

Flow chart 61   Sheet 2 of 3
Notifying compensation events

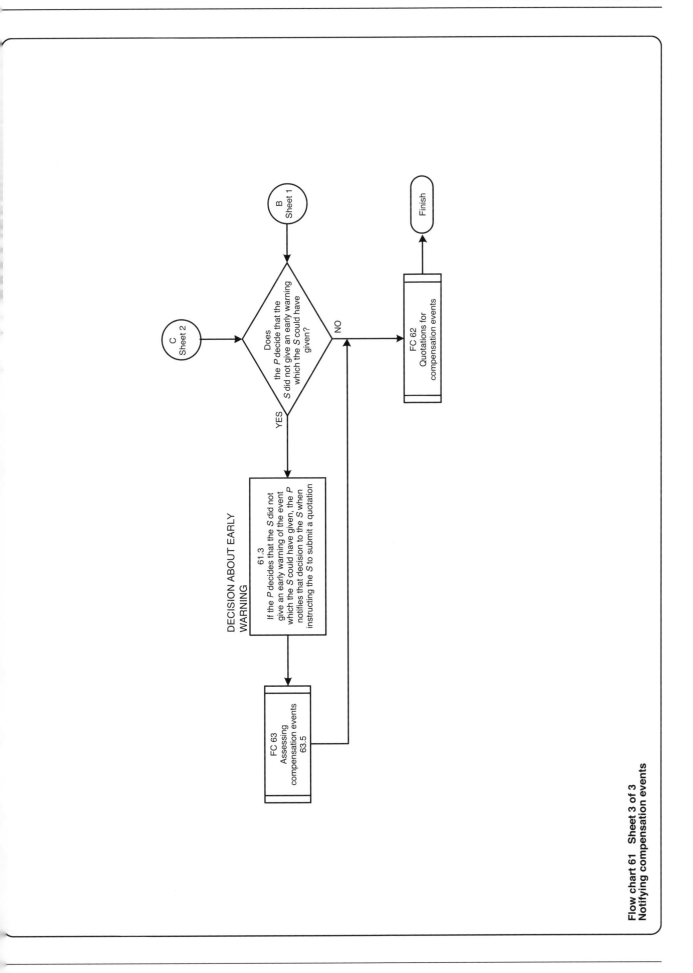

C
Sheet 2

B
Sheet 1

Finish

Does the *P* decide that the *S* did not give an early warning which the *S* could have given?

YES

NO

DECISION ABOUT EARLY WARNING

61.3

If the *P* decides that the *S* did not give an early warning of the event which the *S* could have given, the *P* notifies that decision to the *S* when instructing the *S* to submit a quotation

FC 63
Assessing compensation events
63.5

FC 62
Quotations for compensation events

Flow chart 61   Sheet 3 of 3
Notifying compensation events

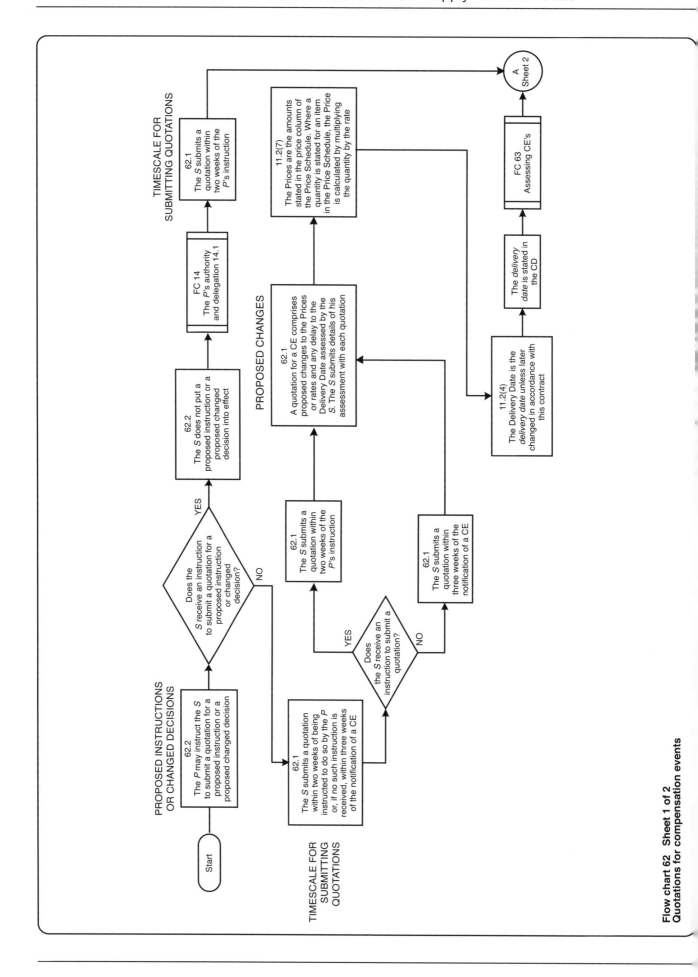

Flow chart 62   Sheet 1 of 2
Quotations for compensation events

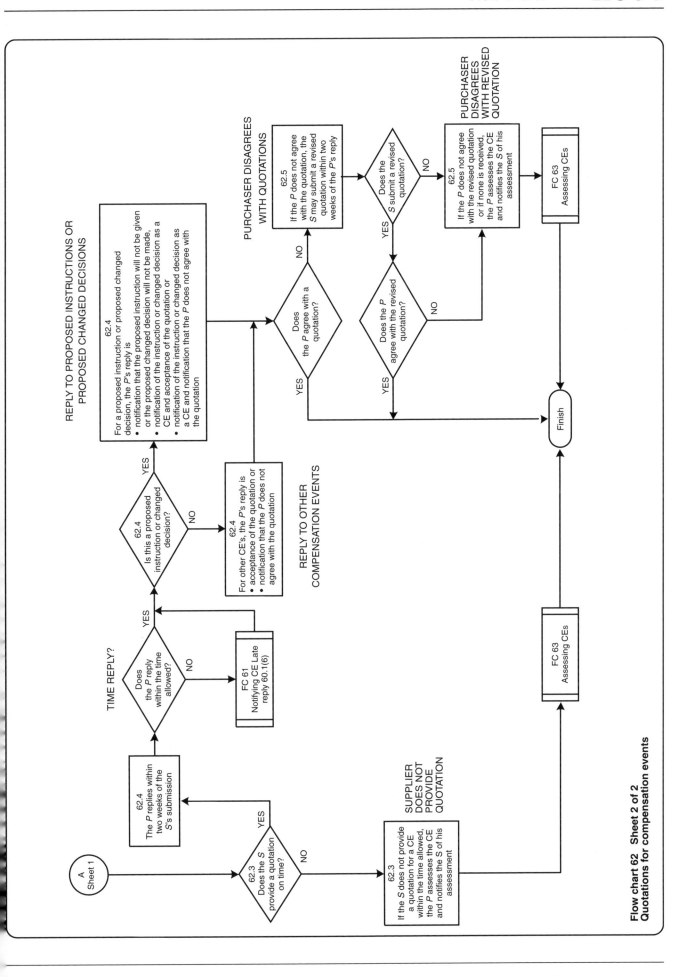

REPLY TO PROPOSED INSTRUCTIONS OR PROPOSED CHANGED DECISIONS

62.4
For a proposed instruction or proposed changed decision, the P's reply is
• notification that the proposed instruction will not be given or the proposed changed decision will not be made,
• notification of the instruction or changed decision as a CE and acceptance of the quotation or
• notification of the instruction or changed decision as a CE and notification that the P does not agree with the quotation

62.4
Is this a proposed instruction or changed decision?

62.4
For other CE's, the P's reply is
• acceptance of the quotation or
• notification that the P does not agree with the quotation

REPLY TO OTHER COMPENSATION EVENTS

PURCHASER DISAGREES WITH QUOTATIONS

62.5
If the P does not agree with the quotation, the S may submit a revised quotation within two weeks of the P's reply

Does the P agree with a quotation?

Does the S submit a revised quotation?

Does the P agree with the revised quotation?

PURCHASER DISAGREES WITH REVISED QUOTATION

62.5
If the P does not agree with the revised quotation or if none is received, the P assesses the CE and notifies the S of his assessment

FC 63 Assessing CEs

TIME REPLY?

Does the P reply within the time allowed?

FC 61 Notifying CE Late reply 60.1(6)

62.4
The P replies within two weeks of the S's submission

A Sheet 1

62.3
Does the S provide a quotation on time?

SUPPLIER DOES NOT PROVIDE QUOTATION

62.3
If the S does not provide a quotation for a CE within the time allowed, the P assesses the CE and notifies the S of his assessment

FC 63 Assessing CEs

Finish

Flow chart 62   Sheet 2 of 2
Quotations for compensation events

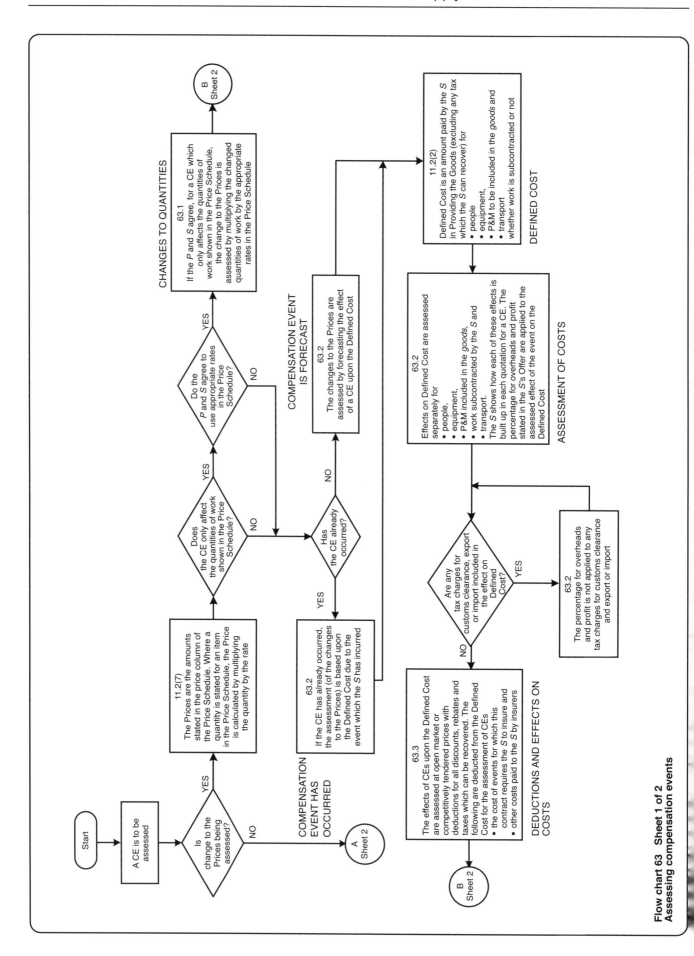

CHANGES TO QUANTITIES

63.1
If the *P* and *S* agree, for a CE which only affects the quantities of work shown in the Price Schedule, the change to the Prices is assessed by multiplying the changed quantities of work by the appropriate rates in the Price Schedule

COMPENSATION EVENT IS FORECAST

63.2
The changes to the Prices are assessed by forecasting the effect of a CE upon the Defined Cost

Do the *P* and *S* agree to use appropriate rates in the Price Schedule?

Does the CE only affect the quantities of work shown in the Price Schedule?

Has the CE already occurred?

COMPENSATION EVENT HAS OCCURRED

11.2(7)
The Prices are the amounts stated in the price column of the Price Schedule. Where a quantity is stated for an item in the Price Schedule, the Price is calculated by multiplying the quantity by the rate

63.2
If the CE has already occurred, the assessment (of the changes to the Prices) is based upon the Defined Cost due to the event which the *S* has incurred

11.2(2)
Defined Cost is an amount paid by the *S* in Providing the Goods (excluding any tax which the *S* can recover) for
• people
• equipment,
• P&M to be included in the *goods* and
• transport
whether work is subcontracted or not

DEFINED COST

63.2
Effects on Defined Cost are assessed separately for
• people,
• equipment,
• P&M included in the *goods*,
• work subcontracted by the *S* and
• transport.
The *S* shows how each of these effects is built up in each quotation for a CE. The percentage for overheads and profit stated in the *S's* Offer are applied to the assessed effect of the event on the Defined Cost

ASSESSMENT OF COSTS

Are any tax charges for customs clearance, export or import included in the effect on Defined Cost?

63.2
The percentage for overheads and profit is not applied to any tax charges for customs clearance and export or import

63.3
The effects of CEs upon the Defined Cost are assessed at open market or competitively tendered prices with deductions for all discounts, rebates and taxes which can be recovered. The following are deducted from the Defined Cost for the assessment of CEs
• the cost of events for which this contract requires the *S* to insure and
• other costs paid to the *S* by insurers

DEDUCTIONS AND EFFECTS ON COSTS

Start

A CE is to be assessed

Is change to the Prices being assessed?

YES

NO

YES

YES

NO

NO

YES

NO

YES

NO

A
Sheet 2

B
Sheet 2

B
Sheet 2

**Flow chart 63   Sheet 1 of 2
Assessing compensation events**

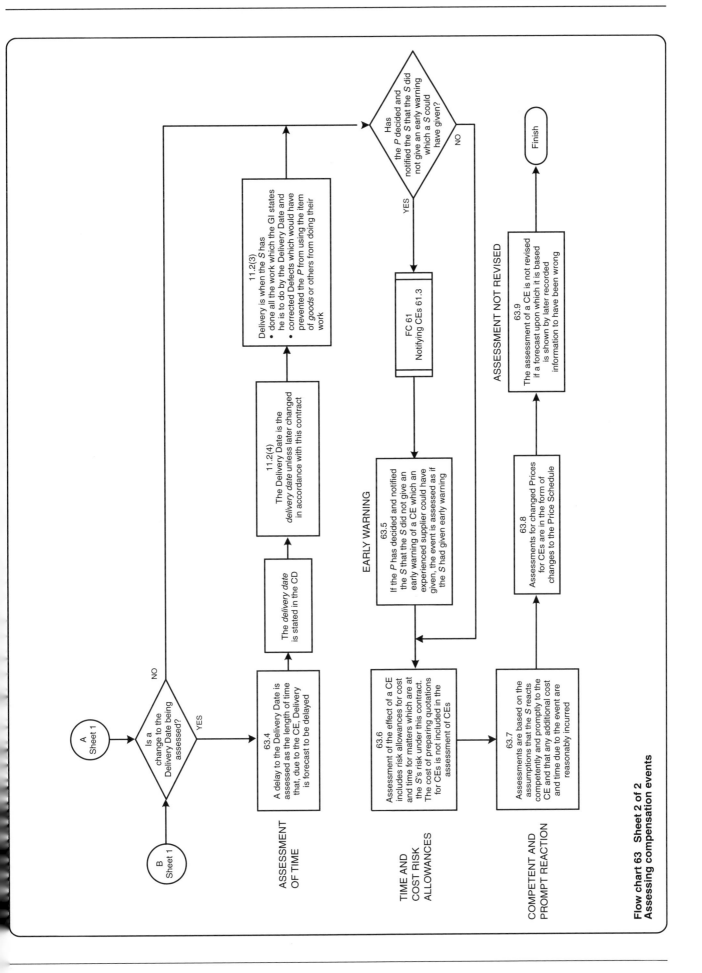

ASSESSMENT OF TIME

63.4
A delay to the Delivery Date is assessed as the length of time that, due to the CE, Delivery is forecast to be delayed

The *delivery date* is stated in the CD

11.2(4)
The Delivery Date is the *delivery date* unless later changed in accordance with this contract

11.2(3)
Delivery is when the *S* has
• done all the work which the GI states he is to do by the Delivery Date and
• corrected Defects which would have prevented the *P* from using the item of *goods* or others from doing their work

Is a change to the Delivery Date being assessed?
NO
YES

A Sheet 1

B Sheet 1

Has the *P* decided and notified the *S* that the *S* did not give an early warning which a *S* could have given?
YES
NO

EARLY WARNING

63.5
If the *P* has decided and notified the *S* that the *S* did not give an early warning of a CE which an experienced supplier could have given, the event is assessed as if the *S* had given early warning

FC 61
Notifying CEs 61.3

TIME AND COST RISK ALLOWANCES

63.6
Assessment of the effect of a CE includes risk allowances for cost and time for matters which are at the *S*'s risk under this contract. The cost of preparing quotations for CEs is not included in the assessment of CEs

COMPETENT AND PROMPT REACTION

63.7
Assessments are based on the assumptions that the *S* reacts competently and promptly to the CE and that any additional cost and time due to the event are reasonably incurred

63.8
Assessments for changed Prices for CEs are in the form of changes to the Price Schedule

ASSESSMENT NOT REVISED

63.9
The assessment of a CE is not revised if a forecast upon which it is based is shown by later recorded information to have been wrong

Finish

Flow chart 63   Sheet 2 of 2
Assessing compensation events

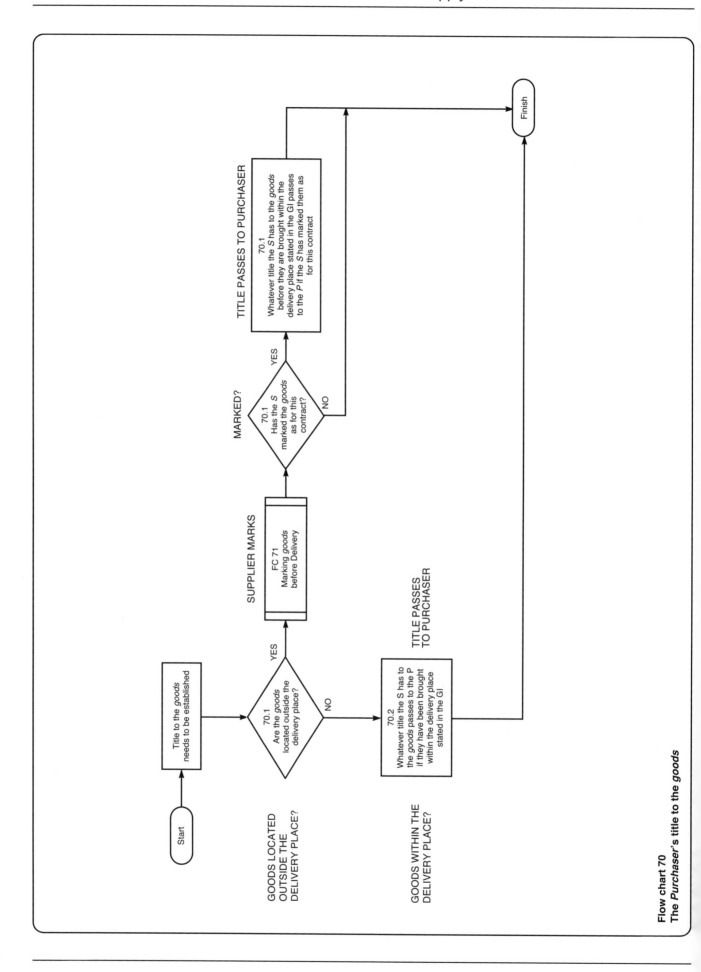

Flow chart 70
The *Purchaser's* title to the *goods*

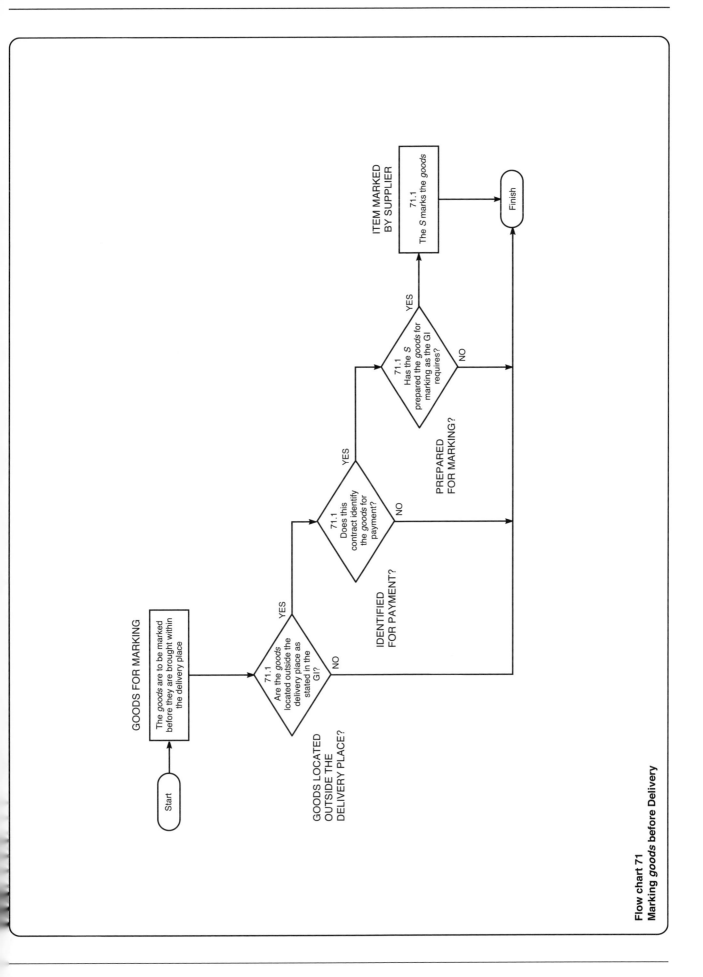

GOODS FOR MARKING

The *goods* are to be marked before they are brought within the delivery place

Start

71.1
Are the *goods* located outside the delivery place as stated in the GI?

GOODS LOCATED OUTSIDE THE DELIVERY PLACE?

YES

NO

71.1
Does this contract identify the *goods* for payment?

IDENTIFIED FOR PAYMENT?

YES

NO

71.1
Has the S prepared the *goods* for marking as the GI requires?

PREPARED FOR MARKING?

YES

NO

ITEM MARKED BY SUPPLIER

71.1
The S marks the *goods*

Finish

Flow chart 71
Marking *goods* before Delivery

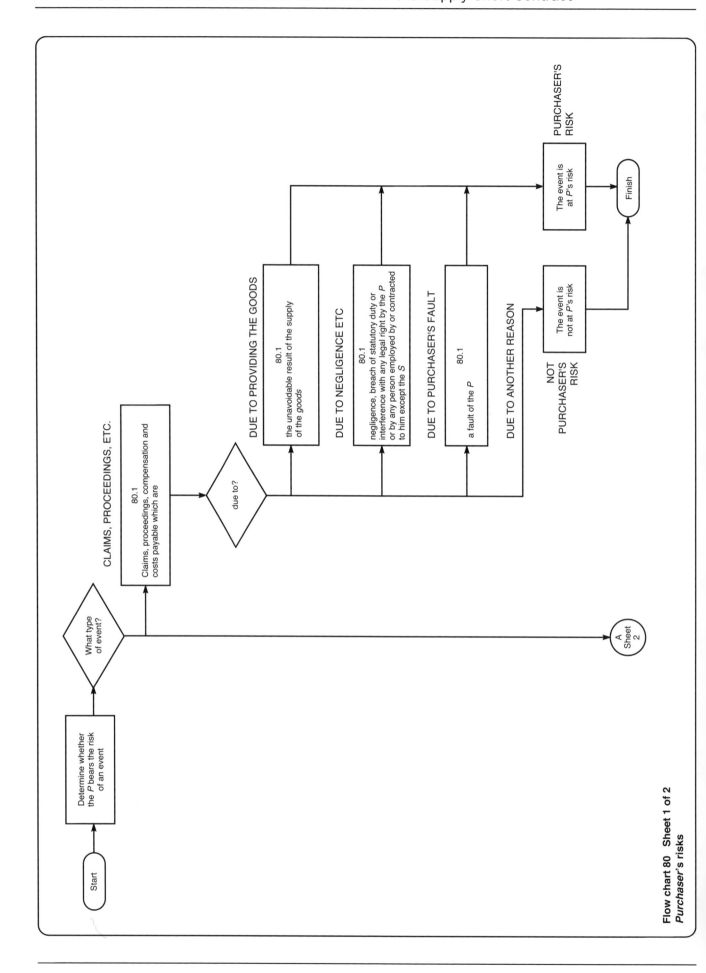

Flow chart 80   Sheet 1 of 2
Purchaser's risks

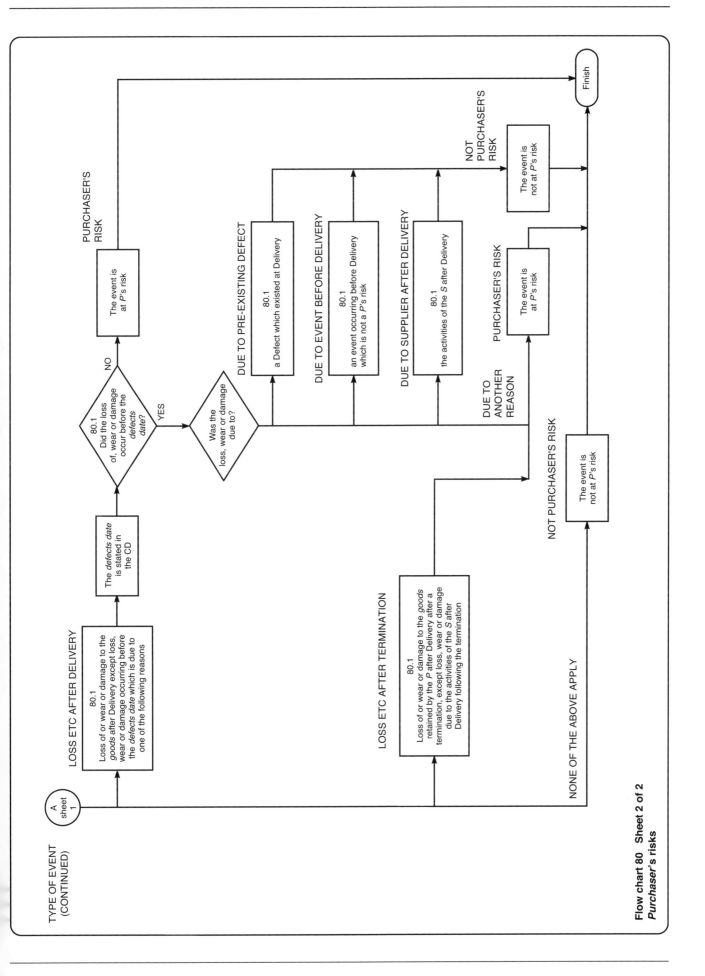

Flow chart 80   Sheet 2 of 2
Purchaser's risks

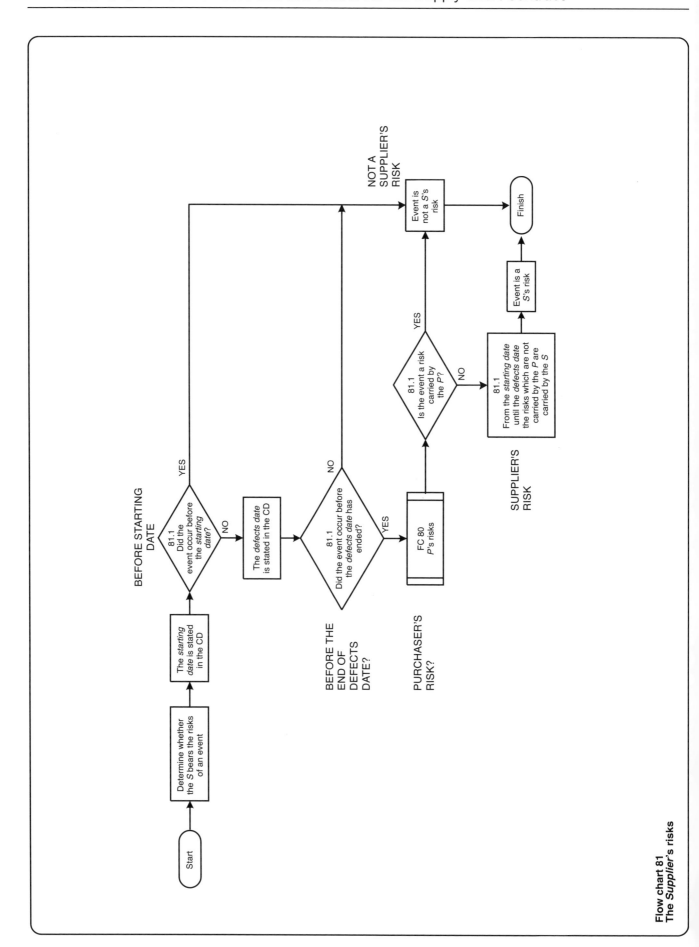

Flow chart 81
The Supplier's risks

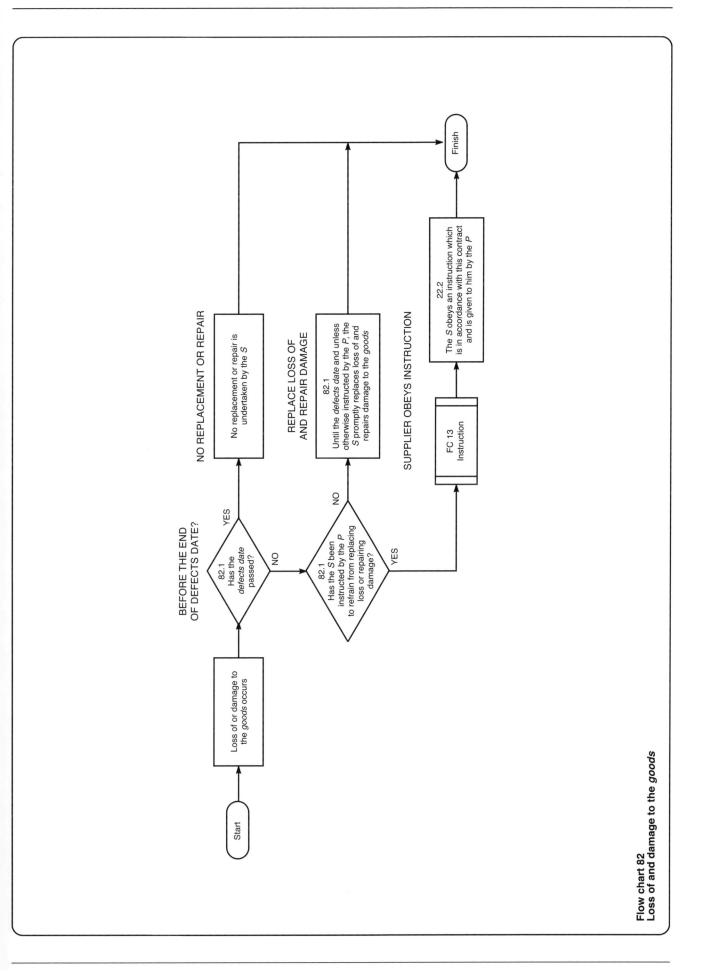

BEFORE THE END
OF DEFECTS DATE?

NO REPLACEMENT OR REPAIR

REPLACE LOSS OF
AND REPAIR DAMAGE

SUPPLIER OBEYS INSTRUCTION

Start

Loss of or damage to
the *goods* occurs

82.1
Has the *defects date*
passed?

YES

No replacement or repair is
undertaken by the S

NO

82.1
Has the S been
instructed by the P
to refrain from replacing
loss or repairing
damage?

NO

82.1
Until the *defects date* and unless
otherwise instructed by the P, the
S promptly replaces loss of and
repairs damage to the *goods*

YES

FC 13
Instruction

22.2
The S obeys an instruction which
is in accordance with this contract
and is given to him by the P

Finish

Flow chart 82
Loss of and damage to the *goods*

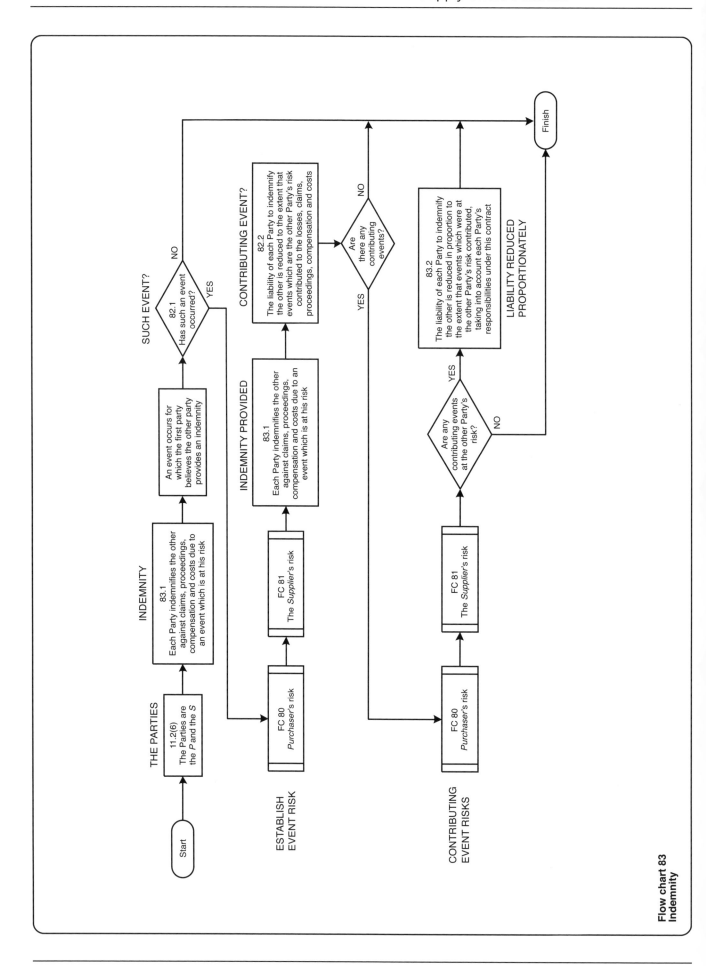

THE PARTIES

11.2(6)
The Parties are the *P* and the *S*

INDEMNITY

83.1
Each Party indemnifies the other against claims, proceedings, compensation and costs due to an event which is at his risk

SUCH EVENT?

An event occurs for which the first party believes the other party provides an indemnity

82.1
Has such an event occurred?

NO

YES

ESTABLISH EVENT RISK

FC 80
Purchaser's risk

FC 81
The *Supplier's* risk

INDEMNITY PROVIDED

83.1
Each Party indemnifies the other against claims, proceedings, compensation and costs due to an event which is at his risk

CONTRIBUTING EVENT?

82.2
The liability of each Party to indemnify the other is reduced to the extent that events which are the other Party's risk contributed to the losses, claims, proceedings, compensation and costs

Are there any contributing events?

YES

NO

CONTRIBUTING EVENT RISKS

FC 80
Purchaser's risk

FC 81
The *Supplier's* risk

Are any contributing events at the other Party's risk?

YES

NO

LIABILITY REDUCED PROPORTIONATELY

83.2
The liability of each Party to indemnify the other is reduced in proportion to the extent that events which were at the other Party's risk contributed, taking into account each Party's responsibilities under this contract

Start

Finish

Flow chart 83
Indemnity

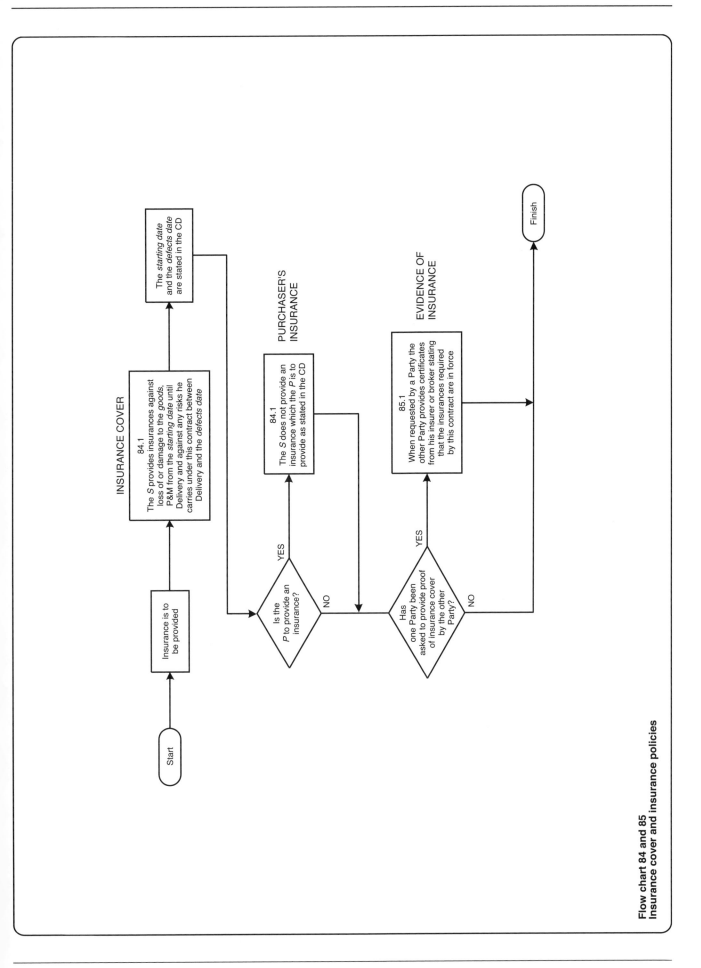

INSURANCE COVER

84.1

The *S* provides insurances against loss of or damage to the *goods*, P&M from the *starting date* until Delivery and against any risks he carries under this contract between Delivery and the *defects date*

The *starting date* and the *defects date* are stated in the CD

Insurance is to be provided

Start

Is the *P* to provide an insurance?

YES

NO

PURCHASER'S INSURANCE

84.1

The *S* does not provide an insurance which the *P* is to provide as stated in the CD

Has one Party been asked to provide proof of insurance cover by the other Party?

YES

NO

EVIDENCE OF INSURANCE

85.1

When requested by a Party the other Party provides certificates from his insurer or broker stating that the insurances required by this contract are in force

Finish

Flow chart 84 and 85
Insurance cover and insurance policies

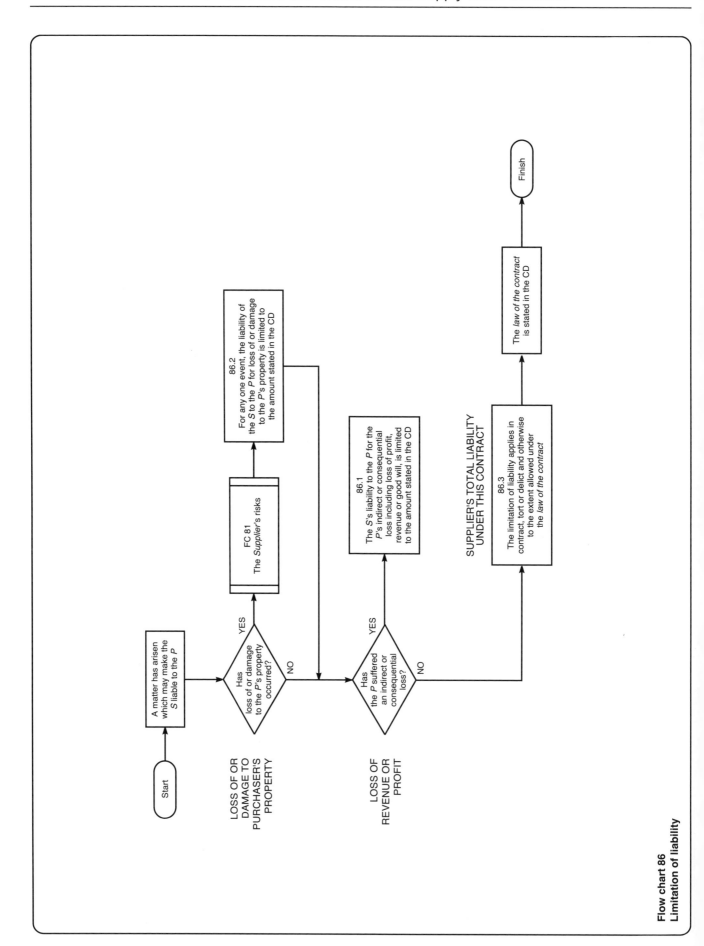

Flow chart 86
Limitation of liability

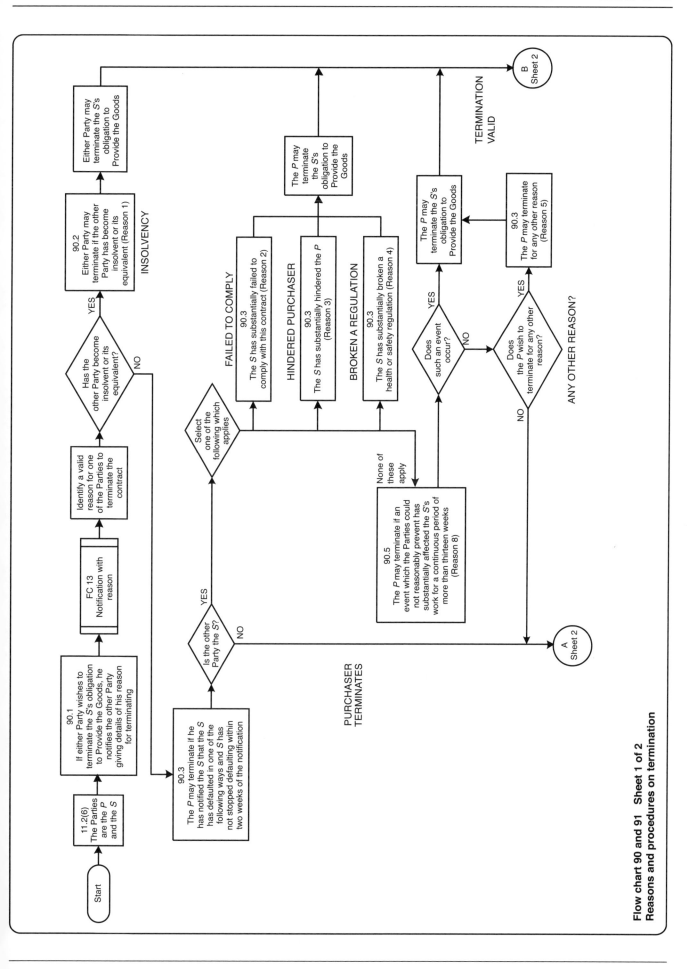

**Flow chart 90 and 91   Sheet 1 of 2
Reasons and procedures on termination**

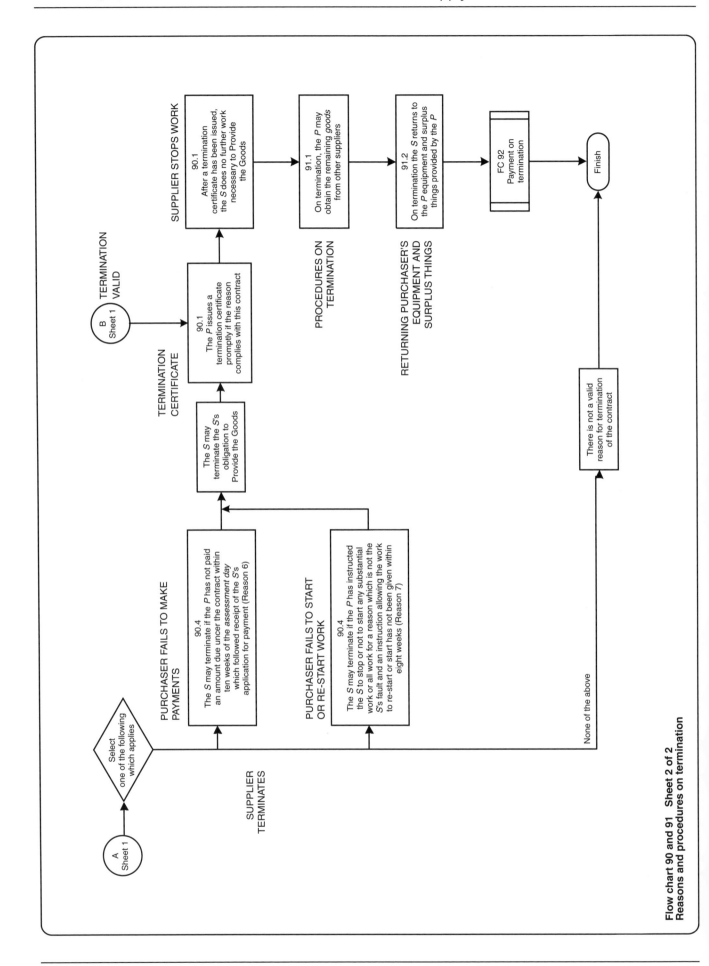

TERMINATION CERTIFICATE

TERMINATION VALID

B
Sheet 1

90.1
The *P* issues a termination certificate promptly if the reason complies with this contract

SUPPLIER STOPS WORK

90.1
After a termination certificate has been issued, the *S* does no further work necessary to Provide the Goods

PROCEDURES ON TERMINATION

91.1
On termination, the *P* may obtain the remaining *goods* from other suppliers

RETURNING PURCHASER'S EQUIPMENT AND SURPLUS THINGS

91.2
On termination the *S* returns to the *P* equipment and surplus things provided by the *P*

FC 92
Payment on termination

Finish

The *S* may terminate the *S*'s obligation to Provide the Goods

PURCHASER FAILS TO MAKE PAYMENTS

90.4
The *S* may terminate if the *P* has not paid an amount due under the contract within ten weeks of the *assessment day* which followed receipt of the *S*'s application for payment (Reason 6)

PURCHASER FAILS TO START OR RE-START WORK

90.4
The *S* may terminate if the *P* has instructed the *S* to stop or not to start any substantial work or all work for a reason which is not the *S*'s fault and an instruction allowing the work to re-start or start has not been given within eight weeks (Reason 7)

There is not a valid reason for termination of the contract

SUPPLIER TERMINATES

Select one of the following which applies

None of the above

A
Sheet 1

**Flow chart 90 and 91   Sheet 2 of 2
Reasons and procedures on termination**

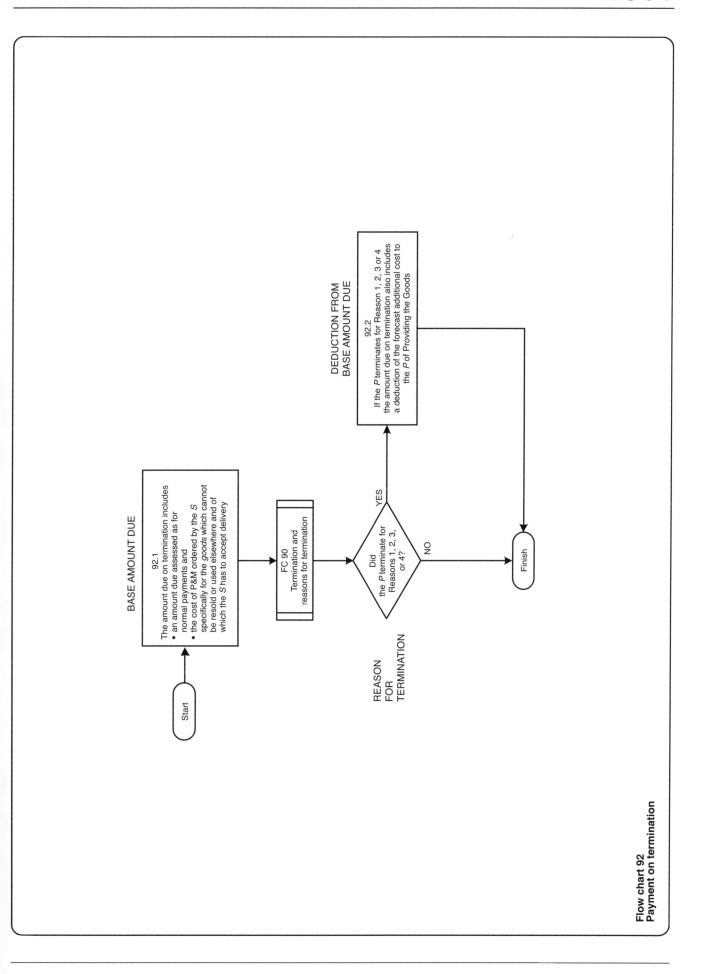

BASE AMOUNT DUE

92.1
The amount due on termination includes
• an amount due assessed as for normal payments and
• the cost of P&M ordered by the *S* specifically for the *goods* which cannot be resold or used elsewhere and of which the *S* has to accept delivery

Start

FC 90
Termination and reasons for termination

REASON
FOR
TERMINATION

Did
the *P* terminate for
Reasons 1, 2, 3,
or 4?

YES

NO

DEDUCTION FROM
BASE AMOUNT DUE

92.2
If the *P* terminates for Reason 1, 2, 3 or 4 the amount due on termination also includes a deduction of the forecast additional cost to the *P* of Providing the Goods

Finish

Flow chart 92
Payment on termination

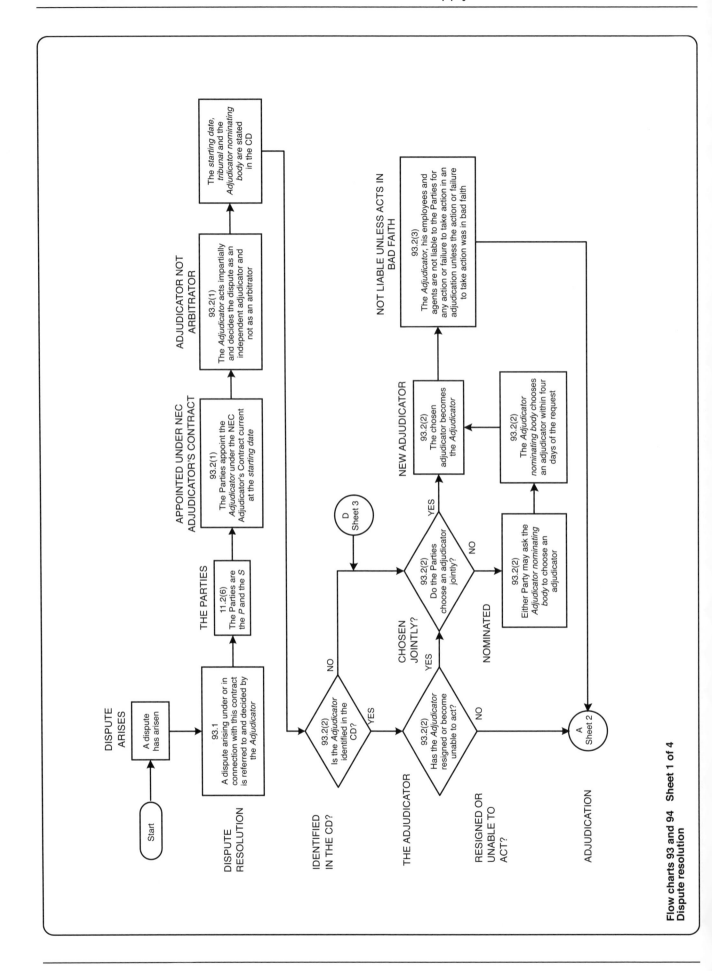

DISPUTE ARISES

Start

A dispute has arisen

DISPUTE RESOLUTION

93.1
A dispute arising under or in connection with this contract is referred to and decided by the *Adjudicator*

THE PARTIES

11.2(6)
The Parties are the *P* and the *S*

APPOINTED UNDER NEC ADJUDICATOR'S CONTRACT

93.2(1)
The Parties appoint the *Adjudicator* under the NEC Adjudicator's Contract current at the *starting date*

ADJUDICATOR NOT ARBITRATOR

93.2(1)
The *Adjudicator* acts impartially and decides the dispute as an independent adjudicator and not as an arbitrator

The *starting date*, *tribunal* and the *Adjudicator nominating body* are stated in the CD

IDENTIFIED IN THE CD?

93.2(2)
Is the *Adjudicator* identified in the CD?

NO

YES

D Sheet 3

THE ADJUDICATOR

93.2(2)
Has the *Adjudicator* resigned or become unable to act?

YES

NO

RESIGNED OR UNABLE TO ACT?

A Sheet 2

CHOSEN JOINTLY?

93.2(2)
Do the Parties choose an adjudicator jointly?

YES

NO

NOMINATED

93.2(2)
Either Party may ask the *Adjudicator nominating body* to choose an adjudicator

93.2(2)
The *Adjudicator nominating body* chooses an adjudicator within four days of the request

NEW ADJUDICATOR

93.2(2)
The chosen adjudicator becomes the *Adjudicator*

NOT LIABLE UNLESS ACTS IN BAD FAITH

93.2(3)
The *Adjudicator*, his employees and agents are not liable to the Parties for any action or failure to take action in an adjudication unless the action or failure to take action was in bad faith

ADJUDICATION

Flow charts 93 and 94   Sheet 1 of 4
Dispute resolution

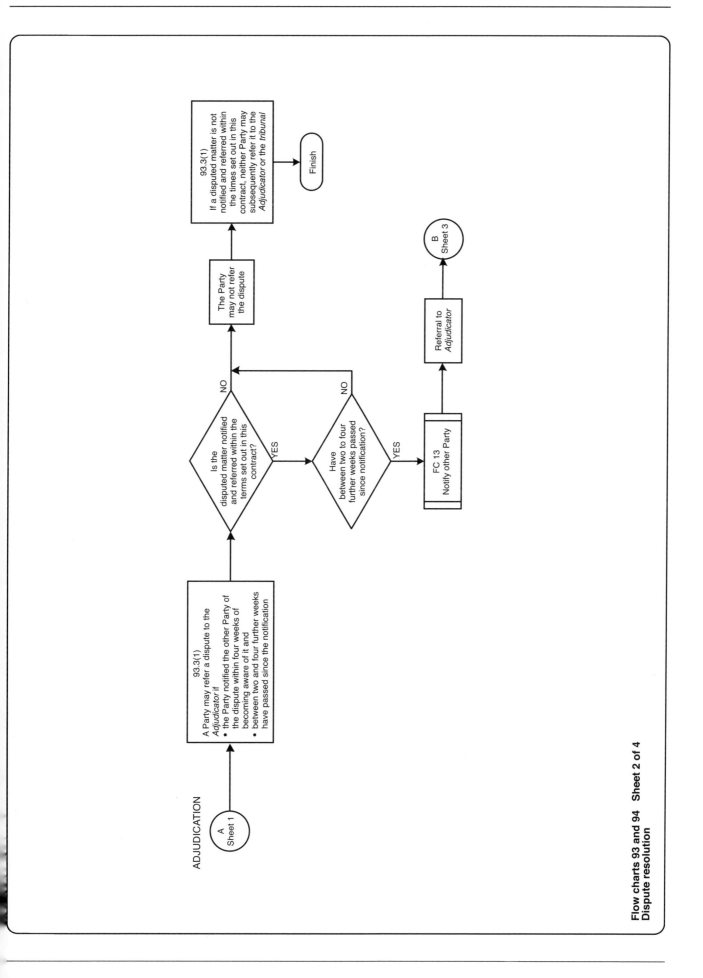

ADJUDICATION

A
Sheet 1

93.3(1)

A Party may refer a dispute to the *Adjudicator* if
• the Party notified the other Party of the dispute within four weeks of becoming aware of it and
• between two and four further weeks have passed since the notification

Is the disputed matter notified and referred within the terms set out in this contract?

YES

NO

Have between two to four further weeks passed since notification?

YES

NO

93.3(1)

If a disputed matter is not notified and referred within the times set out in this contract, neither Party may subsequently refer it to the *Adjudicator* or the *tribunal*

The Party may not refer the dispute

Finish

FC 13
Notify other Party

Referral to *Adjudicator*

B
Sheet 3

Flow charts 93 and 94   Sheet 2 of 4
Dispute resolution

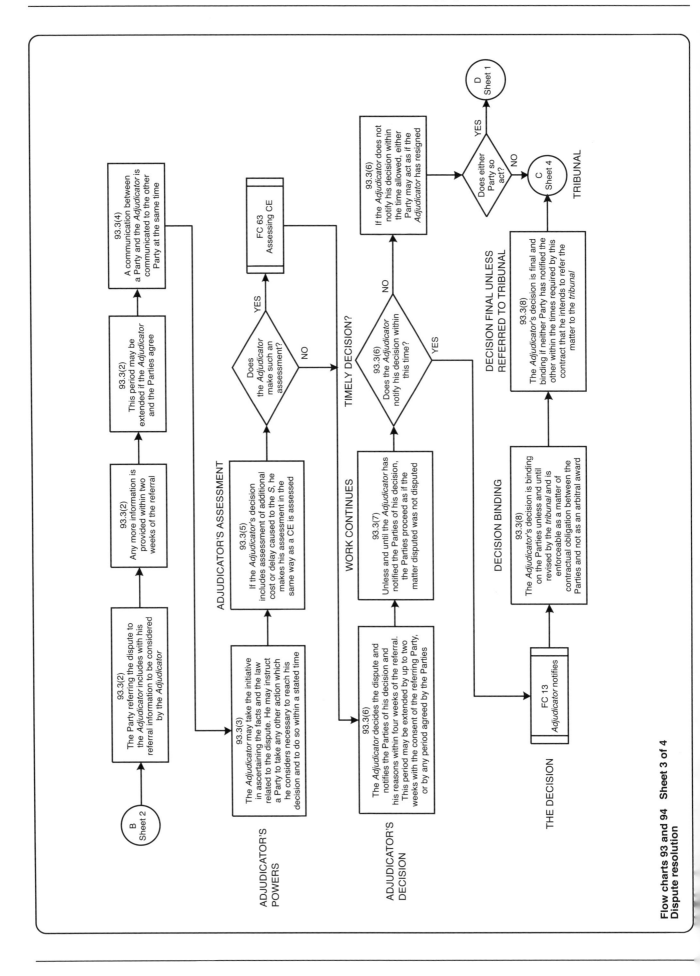

ADJUDICATOR'S POWERS

93.3(3)
The *Adjudicator* may take the initiative in ascertaining the facts and the law related to the dispute. He may instruct a Party to take any other action which he considers necessary to reach his decision and to do so within a stated time

93.3(3)
The Party referring the dispute to the *Adjudicator* includes with his referral information to be considered by the *Adjudicator*

B Sheet 2

93.3(2)
Any more information is provided within two weeks of the referral

93.3(2)
This period may be extended if the *Adjudicator* and the Parties agree

93.3(4)
A communication between a Party and the *Adjudicator* is communicated to the other Party at the same time

ADJUDICATOR'S ASSESSMENT

93.3(5)
If the *Adjudicator's* decision includes assessment of additional cost or delay caused to the *S*, he makes his assessment in the same way as a CE is assessed

Does the *Adjudicator* make such an assessment?

YES — FC 63 Assessing CE

NO

WORK CONTINUES

93.3(7)
Unless and until the *Adjudicator* has notified the Parties of his decision, the Parties proceed as if the matter disputed was not disputed

ADJUDICATOR'S DECISION

93.3(6)
The *Adjudicator* decides the dispute and notifies the Parties of his decision and his reasons within four weeks of the referral. This period may be extended by up to two weeks with the consent of the referring Party, or by any period agreed by the Parties

TIMELY DECISION?

93.3(6)
Does the *Adjudicator* notify his decision within this time?

NO — **93.3(6)** If the *Adjudicator* does not notify his decision within the time allowed, either Party may act as if the *Adjudicator* has resigned

YES

Does either Party so act?

YES — D Sheet 1

NO — C Sheet 4

TRIBUNAL

THE DECISION

FC 13 *Adjudicator* notifies

DECISION BINDING

93.3(8)
The *Adjudicator's* decision is binding on the Parties unless and until revised by the *tribunal* and is enforceable as a matter of contractual obligation between the Parties and not as an arbitral award

DECISION FINAL UNLESS REFERRED TO TRIBUNAL

93.3(8)
The *Adjudicator's* decision is final and binding if neither Party has notified the other within the times required by this contract that he intends to refer the matter to the *tribunal*

Flow charts 93 and 94   Sheet 3 of 4
Dispute resolution

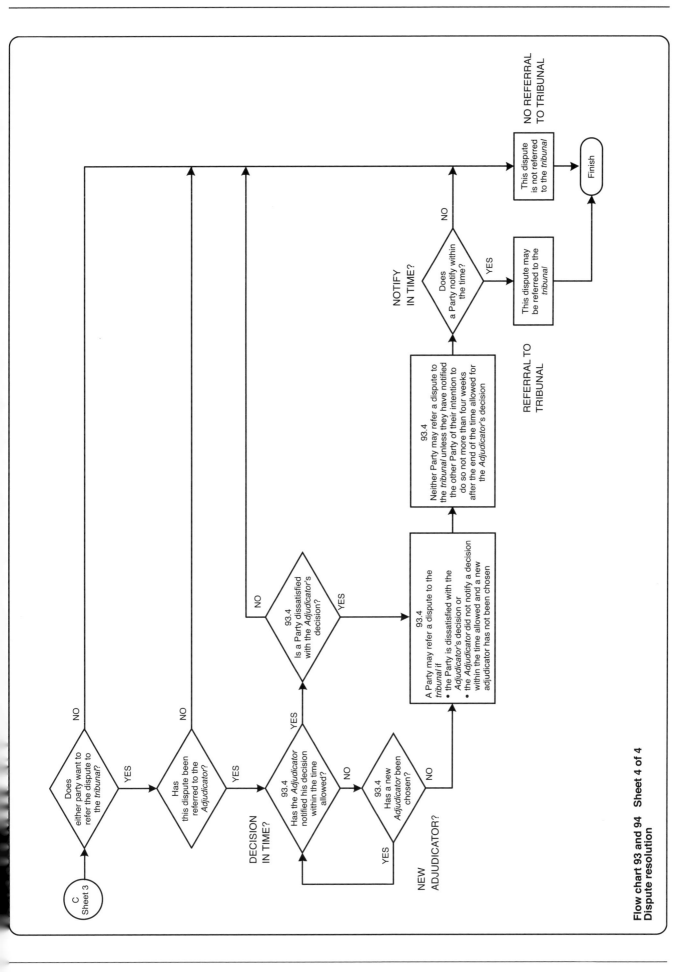

Flow chart 93 and 94   Sheet 4 of 4
Dispute resolution